MW00883166

EXILE

A STORY OF FINDING HOPE

ANTHONY JARRELL

WESTBOW
PRESS®
A DIVISION OF THOMAS NELSON
& ZONDERVAN

All Scripture quotations, unless otherwise indicated, are taken from the Holy
Bible, New International Version®, NIV®. Copyright ©1973, 1978, 1984, 2011
by Biblica, Inc.™ Used by permission of Zondervan. All rights reserved worldwide.
www.zondervan.com The "NIV" and "New International Version" are trademarks
registered in the United States Patent and Trademark Office by Biblica, Inc.™
Scripture marked "KJV" is taken from the King James Version of the Bible.

Author photo by Bailey Thorn Photography

This book is a work of non-fiction. Unless otherwise noted, the author
and the publisher make no explicit guarantees as to the accuracy of
the information contained in this book and in some cases, names of
people and places have been altered to protect their privacy.

WestBow Press books may be ordered through booksellers or by contacting:

WestBow Press
A Division of Thomas Nelson & Zondervan
1663 Liberty Drive
Bloomington, IN 47403
www.westbowpress.com
1 (866) 928-1240

Because of the dynamic nature of the Internet, any web addresses or
links contained in this book may have changed since publication and
may no longer be valid. The views expressed in this work are solely those
of the author and do not necessarily reflect the views of the publisher,
and the publisher hereby disclaims any responsibility for them.

Any people depicted in stock imagery provided by Thinkstock are models,
and such images are being used for illustrative purposes only.
Certain stock imagery © Thinkstock.

ISBN: 978-1-5127-9808-1 (sc)
ISBN: 978-1-5127-9807-4 (hc)
ISBN: 978-1-5127-9809-8 (e)

Library of Congress Control Number: 2017912011

Print information available on the last page.

WestBow Press rev. date: 08/14/2017

This book is dedicated to those who feel like the idea of faith is insane. It's dedicated to the person who feels like life has no meaning or hope. It's dedicated to the person who has been to church but either saw hypocrisy or felt it was too good to be true. It's dedicated to the Christian who feels like they aren't good enough or have missed out on following Jesus.

Go to YouTube and/or Spotify, and search for Exile Book Soundtrack (YouTube channel is Anthony Jarrell) for a playlist of songs I made, which chronologically captures the emotions of the book. These are songs I was listening to in the different seasons of my life (songs listed throughout the book).

Views and opinions expressed in this book are strictly my own and not necessarily representative of Waynesburg University, The Foundry Church, The Assemblies of God, or Southeastern University.

PREFACE

I want to keep this brief. I am an average guy. I am not a celebrity. I'm not an academic genius or an incredible athlete. I've done nothing to be famous. I haven't written this book because I believe I have oracles of wisdom that need to be communicated to the masses. I do not have any magical secrets. I haven't written this book to mimic every self-help book that will be bought just to sit on book shelves all while I'm sent a profit.

I've written this book, part memoir and part commentary, because I believe the experiences of my life are relatable to people. I've written this book because there's nothing "special" about me. I truly believe that our lives and our journeys are so much more and so much bigger than just a few experiences or choices, which is why I've written a book that works through different experiences I've had and what I have struggled with and discovered. At every point, I hope to shed light on the questions I was asking. These questions are essential to this book and what gives this material its value and makes it relatable. I hope you are inspired to constantly ask your own questions and constantly wonder about your own journey and beliefs. Sometimes life is harder to figure out than just happily ever after or black and white. Sometimes life throws curves, and it's difficult to understand much of anything. What this book may or may not capture is the feeling of months and years of circumstances or situations that seemed like they would never end. However, I hope you can relate to these seasons of hopelessness, of longing, of sometimes boredom, through your own similar experiences.

In the hardest moments of my life, which I'll probably go into more detail than I should share, I always wanted to understand the bigger picture so that I could find a way out, heal, and so I could help people never experience what I went through. I found hope that allowed me to make it through and redefine my life, and I want to share that story here. I found something that is timeless. I didn't find understanding through some type of fad or new age idea. I found something that helped me put my whole life in perspective. I found this hope in a story and person that changed everything. My reason for writing is because in my story, I hope you will find a common ground with me. I hope you can discover for yourself how you can have your own story and life redeemed for now and eternity.

CONTENTS

1. What Are We Looking For? 1

2. Belonging 12

3. Turning the Page? 24

4. Jesus..32

5. Starting Over 53

6. What Now 80

7. Found..87

8. All In..92

9. Parting Thoughts - Life More Abundant 102

CHAPTER 1
What Are We Looking For?

The World (and Story) We Live In

Have you ever stopped and wondered what the point of all of this is — is there even a point to any of it? I have a love/hate relationship with running. Some days, I'm into it. Other days, it is the definition of a struggle. I am envious of the people who say they can go running with an empty mind. When I run, it seems to only magnify what is already going on in my head. If it's a great day, then chances are I can feel great when running. The opposite is also true. I say this because I am often trying to make sense of life in between gasping for air in the name of health. For most of my life, I've turned to walks and occasionally running to clear my head and think about life.

I grew up in a small Pennsylvania town, and we lived right on the outskirts. If you turn right from my house, you are "in town." If you turn left, you are in the middle of some of the most beautiful forest backroads and hillsides. Pennsylvania changes drastically with the seasons. There's this long ridge (it's called Bacon Run — no kidding) that loops around my house, and it's a different experience going along it depending on the time of the year. I have had some of the most hopeful and hopeless times along this road. Some moments have felt full of meaning and joy, while others have left me feeling so alone and confused.

Instances like this have caused me to stop when frustrated and question if this is all there is. *Can life ever change? Are we stuck with the cards we are dealt? Are we alone to deal with the pain of life? There's got to be more to life than this.*

I'm talking about how ugly life can be. If you pay attention to the world around you at all, you know what I mean. Hate is a part of daily life for many societies in our world. Politics are rarely used for civil discourse. Social media and TV news outlets are rarely positive about much of anything. Look at the controversial topics of the times, and you instantly have some type of reaction or narrative already in mind. People have strong opinions on everything ranging from drugs to what type of clothing someone should or shouldn't wear.

One of the main themes of this book is that we are all searching for our place to belong. I think it is fair to say we all want to feel loved and accepted. We want to feel like we belong. I think it is easy to see the strain in relationships in today's world. There is division that causes us to be at odds with each other, and it makes us feel like we do not belong. Social media is an interesting creature to figure out. In one sense, we are more connected than ever. You can talk to someone anywhere with a small device. Well, after over a decade of social media's existence, most people recognize the issues we are seeing from it. Much has been written about how we project our best selves online, and we increasingly isolate. Psychologists like Carl Jung would say that we wear masks and perform on the stage of life while internally we suffer because we are not vulnerable. Are we more connected today, or are we given a bigger mask to wear? How can we deal with anything in life if we cannot honestly be ourselves or be known? More specifically, how can we ever find a true sense of belonging if we aren't honest? It's easy to see how that could make cynics out of all of us.

Throw all that in with basic questions about human nature: Why can't we make the world a better place? Why is human history filled with constant war? Why haven't we developed into a peaceful civilization? Why do bad things happen to good people? All of this leads to a tense world to live in. How do we navigate our lives in this crazy mess? What guides us?

We are constantly finger-pointing as a culture, and it's not just Western civilization. How often do we see a group of people blamed for being what is wrong with the world? We see judgment and fear. We see people who believe or act like they are better than others. We see oppression and inequality. We hear hateful talk. We live in a lot of tension. There are serious political questions that need answered without hateful rhetoric. Scientific issues need to be examined with unbiased clarity. We see causes that are meant to bring unity, but they are drawing people apart. We don't see much accountability taken.

Have we ever considered that we could be wrong about how we see the world? I think Michael Jackson was on to something when he sang about looking at the "man in the mirror" and asking him to "make a change." Do we ever look at ourselves in the mirror and wonder if our perceptions or perspectives could be off?

You know when you realize someone isn't as terrible as you thought they were? I knew this guy named Jon in college. When I was a freshman, I constantly saw this older guy around some of my female friends, and he seemed like a sleaze and a tool. He never tried to get to know me out of all the times we were around each other. Then one day on our campus lawn, he said hi to me and asked how I was doing. It turns out that this guy ended up being one of the nicest guys I'd ever met; he was simply a character I had pegged so wrong.

What about the times when you find a deeper issue causing a problem you previously thought you had pinpointed? What if we humbled ourselves and reconsidered the ways we view life? What is the point of anything we do? Is there any purpose to it? Why do we do the things that we do? Why do we buy large houses, save for retirement, etc.? Do we think about what we do? Should we even be doing the things we do? And what is the end goal? What if our goals aren't ultimately satisfying?

I bring up these huge questions because I believe they are essential to our lives. How do we make sense of everything? Where do we belong? Why do we do what we do? I think we try to fit everything into a narrative. We live by trying to make sense of our lives as a story. Have you ever thought about life that way? Maybe you have a family with a lot of history, such as an ancestor who struggled but made opportunities. Doesn't it make sense that such a narrative for your family would be passed down? "We're a tough family, and hard work pays off."

If you or someone you know goes through a tough experience, someone will always say everything happens for reason — such a typical cliché. Of course, we do our best to make sense of experiences based on our knowledge, prior experiences, beliefs, etc. Another example is to look at the importance we place on stories from culture. Everyone has a favorite book, movie, play, moment in history, etc., that speaks to our lives.

These stories are powerful because they matter to us. They help us form an understanding of our lives and our place in this world. What makes something great and memorable is its ability to make you feel something relatable to your own experience. Stories help us understand and feel where we belong. Maybe you've never consciously thought about life and stories this way, but I guarantee that you experience this. We all live by a narrative, and it shapes everything about our lives. I want to share my experiences with you, and I hope to help you discover what narrative is guiding your life — because it changes everything. Maybe you think that life is great because you have everything together, but when you lie down at night (if you are honest with yourself), do you ever truly feel satisfied or sure that you understand everything going on? I don't claim to, but that's exactly my point. Do you feel like you're in the place you're meant to be, or are you always longing for something more? My ultimate hope is that you will discover where you belong and find yourself in the greatest story ever told — the Gospel story.

My Story in a Nutshell

For a good portion of my life, I felt like an exile. Definitions for the word exile typically define it as someone banished or removed from his or her home country or nation. In my case, I would also like to extend that meaning to incorporate one's culture, community, etc. I love this definition I came across once: "The physical or spiritual experience of displacement." For much of my life, I felt as if I did not belong. Many times, I felt as though I had made mistakes that would ruin my life. Many times, I was hurt by people and felt unloved and unwanted. For a long time, I felt I could never quite fit in. At times, I had many casual friends, but I was always jealous of those who seemed to have those inseparable, deep friendships. Sometimes, I wondered whether my life was an accident or if I had so mismanaged my life that I would never measure up. *Am I enough?*

From a young age, I had experiences that caused shame and insecurities. . I wanted people to like me. I didn't want to feel alone. I tried a lot of strategies to try to compensate. I tried to find love in different places like success in sports, girls, looks, popularity, and entertainment. Nothing satisfied or helped me permanently numb the pain. When things went my way, I struggled with letting ego get in the way (yeah...that never ended well.) I have been equally if not worse at, dealing with disappointment. Circumstances led me to go through bouts with loneliness and feeling so insignificant that I wondered if there would ever be a way out. I wondered if a better life, or even just a happy life, was reserved for special people. *Am I not allowed to have a good life?*

I want to be forthcoming about my struggles with depression. In our culture today, there are rising numbers of suspected and diagnosed mental health issues. Many of these are very legitimate. My time working in mental health and in higher-education has granted me front row access to some of the dark realities of the world in which we live. I believe that there are people who claim depression, but they are never truly diagnosed, nor would they likely be in reality. Often times, we mistake genuine sadness for a mental health issue. I say this as a disclaimer because I never saw a physician of any kind for my issues; I was too prideful.

Whether my battles were true depression or merely something related, all I know is what I went through. Several seasons of my life had been marked by periods of what I can best describe as hopelessness. Seasons of feeling nothing. No emotions. No pain. No joy. Nothing. Thinking that I was trapped and unable to escape the mistakes I had made had me thinking I was too insignificant or apathetic to take care of myself. I can remember several seasons and mini-seasons of experiencing this in my life. I never got to the point where I made any type of plan to hurt myself, but it was nice to think about life being out of my hands. I just wanted the pain and nightmare of my life to end. Was there more to life than what I was experiencing?

Faith changed my life. Now hear me out before you anticipate a typical religious spiel. Things like church and the Bible have played a big role in my story, but my experiences are primarily what led me to believe. People would come into my life that encouraged me and helped me feel like I wasn't alone. I would decide to pray because nothing else was working, and I would receive a sense that I wasn't alone. Somehow, I made it through circumstances I thought I wouldn't live through and mistakes I thought would be crippling. These experiences were not smooth sailing by any means, but they helped me understand that I am not alone.

Culture has honestly helped me understand the nature of faith. Different forms of music, literature, films, and not just ones the church would prescribe, have helped me understand that I was longing for something radically different. Was life about more than the rat race or keeping up with the Joneses? Was it possible to have a world where hate didn't exist? A world where everyone was loved, and there was no inequality? Was this world possible, or was there something out of this world that could change our world here?

I grew up believing that *sure, maybe there is a god, but what if there is something to that? What if Jesus is real?* In high school, I began to go to church and read the Bible for myself. I began to learn about this man named Jesus, and my life changed. My struggles changed. People came into my life that helped me feel loved. A whole new world and way of approaching life opened up to me. Things weren't always a breeze. I was far from perfect. I've had (and still have) much to learn. I need to mature as well. People weren't (and aren't) always so loving or genuine. My battles did not (and do not) stop. I came to faith in Jesus because of the changes in my life, and because I believed that somehow this person I was learning about, talking about and praying to was real and always beside me. This hope secures forever. This hope is real and living, and it is found in a man named Jesus. I want to now explain the story of the Bible to you so you understand where I am coming from. Even when I made mistakes and felt like I messed up my life and lost my faith, Jesus never left me. I want to now explain the story of the Bible to you so you understand where I am coming from.

The Gospel

I want to attempt to briefly explain what the accounts of the Bible are. If this is all new to you, I get it. Just work with me here on some things that may be confusing — we'll get there. I'm going to summarize what the majority of Christians have believed for thousands of years and what has been generally documented by historians and theologians. (In the broad narrative, I recognize there are many different perspectives and beliefs on other minor views.) Before we begin, you may of course have preconceived notions about Christians, churches, the idea of God. You may not want to read this part. I understand. God and religion have been misrepresented throughout history (I'll get more into why in a minute.) Perhaps you would call yourself a skeptic, curious of why it is even logical or believable to have faith in any of this. How can there be a God? Why does suffering exist if there is a God? And how can Hell exist if there is a loving God? What about other religions? These are all examples of questions you may have. For starters, resources that I highly suggest will help you answer these are the books *The Reason for God* by Tim Keller, *Mere Christianity* by CS Lewis, *The Case for Christ* by Lee Strobel, as well as anything by Ravi Zacharias and N.T. Wright. (They have helped me become more informed.) Anyway, here is my attempt to summarize the Christian message for the sake of our conversation here.

People of the Christian faith believe the following: There is one God who has always existed in the three distinct persons of God the Father, God the Son (Jesus Christ), and the Holy Spirit. Each of whom is personal in nature. God is infinite, and His nature is not supposed to make sense to our earthly understanding. God divinely inspired human writers to write Holy scriptures which tell His story. We call these scriptures the Holy Bible. It is perfect, and through God's Spirit guiding us, we can interpret it historically, practically, and poetically as He has guided throughout history.

God is the definition of pure love and decides to create the universe. God creates the stars, planets, everything in all of creation. God creates humans in His image. God's design is to have us enjoy all of creation and community with Him forever in perfect harmony. God doesn't create us to be mindless slaves. Adam and Eve, the first humans, are tempted by Satan (a fallen angel who rebelled against God and who waged war against Him and His kingdom). They reject God as King and commit the first sins (acts of disobedience). Therefore, they are banished from the Garden of Eden. Our sin now poisons the once perfect world; we are separated from God our Father because of it. We deserve judgment. Sin brings all sickness, death, disease, hatred, pain and fear into the world. These things were not God's intent for the world. There is not an inch of creation that isn't tainted by sin now. God doesn't plan to leave us as we are in our fallen state. In fact, this is a pattern we see throughout the scriptures and in the real-life testimonies of His people today. God makes a covenant (promise) with His chosen people that He will send a Messiah (the son of God) to redeem our sin, defeat the devil, and restore God's reign over all creation to its' intended state.

The Old Testament of the Bible is filled with stories of God's people longing for Him, rebelling, and subsequently suffering as exiles. God consistently restores their nation and never forsakes His people. God gives Moses the Ten Commandments (laws for the people to keep). The laws ultimately are practical and meant to protect us. Some examples are, "Do not steal, do not kill, and do not create a God of something that shouldn't be." The issue is, because of sin, we cannot possibly ever live up to it, so sacrifices were made to atone for forgiveness of sins. God's people go through periods of exile, but they eventually return home to Jerusalem. The Old Testament ends with God's people living essentially as exiles in their home under the rule of the Roman government. This sets the stage in the New Testament for everything to change.

Jesus Christ (the Son of God) is born into the world by a virgin woman named Mary to very humble circumstances. He is essentially on a divine rescue mission. As 100% God and 100% man, He lives a perfect, sinless life. Jesus begins His public ministry as an adult. He proclaims Himself as the promised Messiah through His teachings, miracles, and loving the most outcast and sinful people. His message is so counter-cultural and selfless that it causes tension to this day. The Roman government fears a societal uprising due to the exploding movement surrounding this Jesus, not to mention the corrupt Jewish Pharisees who believe He is a heretic. Jesus is murdered by public crucifixion on a cross. Jesus rises from the dead three days later. His death and resurrection is the atonement (paying the price) for humanity's sin. The resurrection vindicates His entire mission and confirms that He is indeed God as He conquers sin and death. We now have hope and confidence in Him for eternity. Jesus reappears to His disciples and gives them the Great Commission: A plan to join with Him in making disciples (followers), so He can build His church (God's family). Jesus says He must go so that the Holy Spirit can come to live in and through His people, empowering and guiding.

God's people are like sojourners (refugees or aliens) in this world but also citizens in the Kingdom of God. Followers of Jesus are tasked with leading others to a saving relationship with Jesus and working to bring restoration to this broken world (bringing the Kingdom of Heaven to Earth) until one day Jesus returns for His people and to complete this process. God will make all things new — a new Heaven on Earth. God's people will be resurrected and joined together. There will be no more pain, death, or sin in this new Heaven. Everything we have enjoyed in life will now be infinitely more perfect and amazing, and greatest of all, we will be reunited in perfect community with our creator, God. Our ultimate satisfaction, fulfillment, and joy is and will be made complete when we have eternity with Him. Those who have rejected God will be separated forever with the devil in Hell.

This is my retelling of the narrative of the Bible. I realize there are questions in life we will always have. No one has the answer to every question in life. The Gospel helps me make sense of why there is pain and suffering in the world. Sin is the reason, I believe, that there are things like death, racism, poverty, war, and all forms of suffering. In the scriptures, I see a God who never leaves me, even in the worst of times. I can have hope in something and someone bigger than anything I am going through.

We all have a choice to make in our lives. The scriptures say that we all have sinned. In the New Testament, for example, the Bible states, "We need to repent of our sinful ways and receive Jesus as our savior." (Romans 10:9) We are saved by our faith, but we enter a relationship that is ongoing. Faith is more than a one-time decision. The Gospel is not about a God who wants to keep us away from anything good or make us lead boring lives, but about a God who wants us to join the adventure we were created to be a part of. I would suggest the book *Multiply* by Francis Chan as a great resource to anyone looking to better understand the ideals of scripture.

When we engage with this narrative, this reality of our existence, it changes everything about our own story. We find our place of belonging. I have stated some simple perspectives on our world, an overview of my story, and a summary of the Gospel so that as I tell my story in detail, you will hopefully see my life as I have experienced it. My hope is that you will find it relatable. I hope you will experience that God's love extends forever to all of us exiles. Again, I don't write this because I think I have anything new or important to add to theological or cultural arguments. My goal is solely for you to be moved by my story, the most original thing I can share, and that you, too, will experience Jesus in your own life. Thank you for walking this journey with me.

CHAPTER 2
Belonging

I grew up in a very small Pennsylvania town of maybe a thousand people. My dad is a retired coal miner and worked different truck driving jobs between coal mining positions. Our socioeconomic status changed with the ups and downs of my dad's job transitions. My mom worked most of my childhood as an office manager for a small automobile junkyard before moving into local government later in my teenage years. The energy industry runs deep in my family; my grandfather was a coal miner, my one uncle is a mining engineer, and my cousin owns a successful gas and oil supply company.

My younger brother Alan and I lived the lives of a pair of classic '90s kids. Our area is typically one of the more impoverished areas in the state, but we were lucky to have access to developing TV and internet companies. We didn't grow up around very many other kids, and there wasn't much to do in our town. We went to a small elementary school where each grade had about twenty kids. To present day, I still feel a strong bond with the group I grew up with. My family had a big backyard where we could throw balls, build bonfires, and play with our pets. We also live close to some incredible woods, which were nice for hiking and hunting.

My brother and I loved all things entertainment because of our limited play options. We owned just about every video game system that came out in the 90s and 2000s: A N64, the first two generations of PlayStation, a Dreamcast, Nintendo's GameCube, the first Xbox, and then a 360 and so on. I loved anything and everything on TV. If it was a '90s or early 2000s cartoon, I was all about it. Pokémon, Dragon Ball Z, Nickelodeon and Cartoon Network — all of it. I was exposed to so many movies as a kid as well. I quickly became obsessed. Of course, being born in 1991, I was addicted to all things Disney—The Lion King is still the greatest. I moved on to loving classic and current action movies. I also loved all the "kid-friendly" music that came out in the late '90s — Backstreet Boys, N-Sync, and even Britney Spears, (Look, I was like 7, okay?) I loved entertainment, and it allowed me to have a wild imagination. As a kid, I would often just go hang out outside and walk around, dreaming up stories in my head. Technology advances for my generation allowed me to be exposed to so much of the world, but I appreciated every new development. Life felt like it was constantly getting better as a kid, but it was hard to take much for granted because I also saw how rough life could be, too. My family worked incredibly hard to provide for all of us. After all, my dad's profession forced him to crawl around in tight spaces in wet, sub-zero temperatures, all in total darkness to make ends meet.

I felt so loved as a kid. My family is huge on my mother's side and very close. I never really knew my dad's family. I grew up a mile from my mom's parents, and the majority of my aunts and uncles always lived close. My family was always there for me. This one time when I was five, I was outside at my grandparents' house. The neighbors had apparently been playing the game of croquet earlier, and one of them was now mowing the yard. So, he hit one of the old, metal croquet goals, and it launched probably half a football field over into my grandparents' yard. This goal hit me in my left leg below my knee, created a gash, and fractured the bone. My family dropped everything to make sure I was taken care of. This crazy experience helped me realize as a young kid that family is always there for you. Even though my family has the normal quirks and problems, I never doubted that we loved each other and everyone belonged.

Even strangers were welcome in my family. Some of my best memories are from holidays. Every Christmas, for example, would be spent at my grandparents' house. Everyone would pile together in this little house just off the interstate surrounded by pine trees and snow on the ground, eating, telling great stories, and playing cards for hours. In hindsight, I don't think it could've been any more picture perfect. My grandparents, Bill and Ruth, taught me what real love looks like. They may have been wild in their younger years, but I knew them in their late 60s and 70s, and they were the sweetest people I'd ever known. My grandmother was the stereotypical Italian grandmother — I could not leave her house until I ate something. They would have done anything for my brother Alan and me. They loved to be that complaining old couple, but I saw their true hearts in how they loved others. My grandfather was a volunteer firefighter for over 50 years, and my dad was one for 30. They felt a need to take care of people, and they would open their home to those who didn't have anyone. At Christmas, neighbors, friends from all over town, and sometimes just random people would come over. Everyone had a place at the table, plenty of food to share, and a chance to be hustled in cards by my grandfather. (Seriously, the guy never lost.) I've seen this emphasis on caring for others passed down to my parents, aunts, uncles, cousins, everyone. My family has always wanted to make sure everyone felt loved and belonged, even with their differences of opinion.

Earlier I mentioned that I went to a small elementary school. As a young kid, I didn't have those "best friends" that some kids often have, but my elementary class was special. I have good memories of everyone being friends with everyone else. These were the days when you would have a pizza or pool party and the entire class would be invited. I don't recall much of the teasing or fights or any of those things that typically come along with young children. We felt like a family in many ways. I loved our elementary teachers; they really loved us, too, and we knew it. I will forever be grateful for these exceptional people.

Anyway, our teachers would let us do the craziest things — stuff that no school would allow today. Recess all day? Why not! My 5th grade teacher would take us out behind the school, and we would hike in the woods when the weather was okay. We made cardboard rocket ships and flew them. We churned and cooked apple butter in a giant cauldron — believe me, don't knock it till you've tried it. Our teachers cared about us and valued us. We kids did everything together. Every experience felt like being a part of something special because we shared life. It didn't matter if it was trading Pokémon cards, reading Harry Potter, starting an elementary football team, or going to the movies, everyone felt like they belonged. I was a very awkward kid, usually day dreaming and terribly uncoordinated when it came to sports. None of that mattered though, because we loved each other.

Middle School

(Playlist songs 1-3)

My life changed when I made it to middle school. See, when I started 6th grade, my only option was to be bused a half-hour north to a larger town for middle and eventually high school. For an eleven-year-old, it was culture shock: There were roughly 500 students at this new school, and it worked on a typical change-classrooms-every-period format. I did fine academically, but everything changed socially. It proved difficult for me to make friends in school. I was always the youngest kid in my grade, and I think my maturity developed a little slower, and it really hurt me. My elementary friends all seemed to make friends relatively easily and had little use for me. They were friends with the cool kids now.

A lot proved to be very scary. Our school was still small by most standards, and we could interact with all three grade levels. I was exposed to things I wasn't ready for. Not only were older kids in relationships, but dating also began in my grade. To take things a step further, it seemed everyone talked about having sex. I felt the need to fit in, so I tried, in spectacularly unsuccessful fashion, to flirt with girls. I did not have the slightest clue how to talk to a girl. I very quickly was introduced to drugs. In the sixth grade, the people who accepted me the most were a rougher crowd. I was first offered drugs that year, but I declined every offer. I didn't care much about people's social standing. I came from the school where we were equals, but I quickly learned that I didn't want to be in the wrong crowd and be in trouble. So, I tried to make friends with more of the "in" crowd.

I became an easy target to make fun of. I wasn't a "cool" kid, but I wanted desperately to belong. A few of my friends from elementary school allowed me to still hang around them, and I tried to maintain those relationships since, well...I didn't exactly have other options. I became known as "Jockstrap" to these guys because I "was always attached to them." Great first impression at the school. I was mad fun of for the clothes I wore. My parents were great at saving money, and there were times when money was really tight, so sometimes, I would only get a few outfits for school. I was labeled as a poor kid for a while and mocked. Apparently, poor equals uncool in middle school logic. I was called "grub" often. I'll never forget specific instances of being made fun of for the clothes I wore.

Several times I was chastised and referred to as being gay. For instance, I still had the cheesy little boy haircuts. That was a common target. I never did anything to actually make people think I was gay, but I suppose to middle school guys and girls in the early 2000s, being gay was the worst thing you could be. Middle school was showing itself to be a nasty place. I quit the football team because practice usually turned water breaks into spitting-on-Anthony games. Peers told me, "gays can't play football."

Middle school also became a physically dangerous place. I never knew when I was going to be randomly shoved, have books knocked out of my hands, or even be hit. It seemed like sport to hurt me. One time at a party, a random game broke out where I believe the objective was to knock me down and kick me in a circle until they got bored. I would cower in fear, thinking people were going to hit in the most random moments. I had been conditioned to fear.

I hated going to school. I dreaded every second of it. I did not want to involve myself in anything. I wanted to be invisible. At the same time, I hated being that way. I wanted to be a part of the "in" crowd and have friends and do things. I loved sports, and I dreamed of playing something again, but the bullying only continued to get worse. Middle school seemed to be filled with two types of kids: Those who wanted to cause me pain and those who were either indifferent/had no interest in getting to know me. At least all the people who hurt me cared that I existed. In a plot twist, several of the people who would bully me started to get to know me and somewhat befriended me. A few of these guys would get mad and defend me if other people tried to pick on me. I had developed trust and relationships with my abusers. People...this is the definition of Stockholm Syndrome.

I learned that there is such a thing called the social ladder. It depended on what you could offer. Are you from a rich family and have nice clothes? Are you great at sports? Are you smart? Are you funny? Congratulations, because that (apparently) gives you value. I should like you if you meet one of these qualifications. It's sad to think, but I don't believe most people in our society grow out of this perspective. What if you are just a person? Do you have value? Why is it that we seem to get our sense of value from others?

I love the book *Searching for God Knows What* by Donald Miller. In one part, he explores these questions in relation to human's relationship with God broken by sin. In Genesis 3, we see that Adam and Eve experience shame for the first time by sinning. They subsequently lose their identity in their relationship with God, and so begins the struggle to fill insecurities with all sorts of things (others, money, sex, etc.). I was a kid wanting to find anything to feel loved or important.

Many people adapt and do things they dislike to win the approval of others. I would be quilted into doing ridiculous things for the humor of others. This was about the time that shows like *Viva La Bam* and anything involving Johnny Knoxville were popular, so doing things that were dangerous was funny to others. *Am I a dancing monkey?* I'd be forced to do people's homework, sometimes buy food for others, and just generally be an embarrassment. Admittedly, this story is funny in retrospect now, but it's a classic example of middle school. One time I was walking back to my table in the lunch room when I noticed everyone seemed to be acting weird. I came back and opened my binder to find that an entire bowl of baked beans had been poured inside. All my notes and homework was ruined. My friend James at least saved my calculator for me. I was a laughingstock.

Like many memories from middle school, I've tried to block this next one out. Please skip ahead if you are uncomfortable with graphic stories. I don't remember much from this next story, other than I think it was in the 7th grade. I was staying the night with a few people. Late at night everyone had fallen asleep, but I was still up talking with one of the kids I knew. Eventually he started telling me these stories about sex with girls and different fantasies he had. I was not particularly intrigued until he was talking about girls at our school. Then I was invested. He reaches in his bag and shows me pornography for the first time. The tide turned, and he started asking me if I wanted to do anything. I had no interest and tried to get out of the situation.

Eventually he threatened me and forced me to use my hand on him in a sexual act.

He wanted me to do more, but I refused, and spent half the night locked in the bathroom. I was so scared. *Why did I let that happen? Am I gay? How can I live with myself?* I never told anyone about this. I wanted it to go away.

I know that there are millions out there who encounter even worse horrors with sexual abuse. Nothing about that fact diminishes the pain it caused me. I lived in fear of not only physical abuse, but what if I could be raped? Many male peers had perverse senses of humor and would joke around, threatening to sexually assault each other. *What if that happened to me?* My fears and experiences, if anything, have helped me relate to the awful horrors so many live with.

Anyway, the kid and I never spoke a word about it. The nightmare was not over for me though. I was intrigued by the porn. It was frightening and made me sick to my stomach to see it, but it also felt like it was everything I ever wanted. This began an addiction to lust that would haunt me for a long time. Porn became my drug of choice.

Coping

(Playlist songs 4-5)

Here I was, first twelve and then thirteen years-old, and my life felt like a daily nightmare. Every day going to school was frightening. Who was going to hurt me today? What was going to embarrass me today? Like I mentioned earlier, the best possible outcomes would be if I was given the grace of being invisible, or — on the best days — had a couple positive conversations. I hated this way of life. I wanted to be liked by people. I wanted to play sports beside my peers. I couldn't help but feel perpetually inadequate. I didn't think things could get any better. Everyone and everything made me feel like I didn't belong.

There have been studies done in the education world that show how teachers show preference or treat students differently based on expectations or experience. I did fine in school, but I tried my best to not be the center of attention. I picked up on being treated as if I was lesser or didn't have the same potential as others.

I never had the courage to tell anyone. I assumed my parents were out of touch with my issues. No way they would understand the context. Not only that, but I believed if I reached out to get help, things would only get worse. I dreaded going to the bathroom in middle school. It was like walking into a UFC cage. Our building was an old multi-floor facility with long stairwells and isolated bathrooms. There were plenty of places to be roughed up by somebody, and I knew that too well. Strangely, there was a part of me that wanted to be tough. Being a crybaby would have only made me suffer more, or at least that's what I believed. During middle school, I started to develop a love for professional wrestling (the "fake stuff," WWE), and it made me want to have courage. I would get so wrapped up in the stories. Even in the worst of times, I knew I could tune in on a Monday night and vicariously enjoy the "competition theater" if you will.

Pro wrestling is just one example of things I used to cope through isolating and pretending I was fine. My parents had no idea things were so bad. Sure, they probably thought I was stressed at times, but I would venture to guess my family thought I was a lazy kid with no ambition. To be fair, there was an element of truth to that, but I was never honest. I never tried drugs or alcohol as a means of coping. Even though I was developing an addiction to pornography, I never tried to have sex with any of my peers. I wanted everyone to think I was a good kid, and deep down, I wanted to be. Besides, the "bad" kids didn't seem to be any better off than I was. Maybe it was the Stockholm Syndrome (which I still don't know if I mean that facetiously or not), but I never wanted anyone to be hurt that hurt me. I liked many of these people and saw good in them. Sure, I would get angry, and sometimes, in the worst of moments, wish people would be hurt, but I simply just wanted to be liked by people. I was never tempted to be one of those kids who went postal. I thought that if I just held out long enough, eventually things would get better. I think I'm not alone in this view. I think a lot of people live their lives thinking that if we just ignore our issues, they will just go away. I am not so sure about that, but it was my main strategy back then.

I know that in this time (and even through high school), I tried to change so much of my life to fit in. I didn't go to every extreme, but I know I sacrificed things I was naturally interested in to try to fit in. I sacrificed focusing on being a good student or pursuing ways in which I was naturally creative. For instance, I never once considered joining theater or band. Even though these were things I probably would have naturally been drawn to, I did not want to do anything to become a further target of humiliation. If anything, being humiliated caused me to be more self-aware. I would still be the kid who was a little weird. Still, I know that I had a loss of innocence at an age far younger than anyone should have to. I know years of childlike imagination and creativity were lost to fear. I was in an environment of pressure, where there seemed to be these coexisting expectations where you either had to be the best at something, you had to be beautiful, you had to have the girl, or you had to go after things like drugs, or things like being a fighter. I was none of these things. I felt forgotten, like I didn't belong.

I worked into a good rhythm of isolating and pretending I was fine. Like I mentioned, I did fine in school, but I didn't have much motivation. I developed an addiction to video games, and my brother and I would spend most our time after school playing things like *Halo* or sports games. I had plenty of friends who enjoyed video games, so it helped me build rapport. I loved all the sports I could make time for, so I also started to become quite the sports statistics nerd. I loved building and developing teams on different sports video games. We lived not far away from West Virginia University, so my uncle Dan would take me to football and basketball games. This was at a time when WVU's athletics programs were thriving nationally, so this fandom had become a positive influence in my life. I slowly created this little world of video games obsession, sprinkled with sports and pro wrestling spectatorship. I was addicted to eating unhealthily (Coca-Cola was my soulmate), and this only perpetuated my laziness. I was a couch potato at thirteen. It worked for me and kept me distracted from all the pain.

I developed an appreciation for music at this time. This was the early 2000s, so I got into popular hard rock. (Rap didn't do it for me then.) I'd listen to stuff like P.O.D., Creed, Switchfoot, and Breaking Benjamin. I'd see music videos for bands like this on MTV (RIP), and I recognized that the lyrics dealt with some pretty heavy material — things like suicide, pain, and fear. This music seemed to also point to hope in the midst of all of that. I didn't know why, but this resonated with me, and I wasn't aware at the time that many of these bands were singing about faith and spiritual issues. I also went through a pretty big classic rock phase in middle school and into high school. I'd listen to stuff like Van Halen, Phil Collins, U2, etc. Those songs, however cheesy some are, were usually thematic and story-centered in nature. These types of music resonated because they gave me hope that maybe there would be a resolution, a plot twist to all the pain I was going through. Maybe in time, things would change; maybe I would find where I belonged.

Things did not get any better over time. By the time I was in 8th grade, I was becoming an ugly kid. I had been desensitized to a lot. I had never processed anything or had been honest to anyone. School was the same. Many peers swore profusely, so I did, too. I wanted to be funny, so I developed the same twisted sense of humor everyone else had. I would say truly heinous things because I wanted to be "cool," to be "bad." Sex was becoming an increasingly bigger temptation for everyone, so combined with my lust for porn, I was feeling pressure to pursue that. I was by no means just a victim during this time. I did many ugly things. I had become a pretty selfish person. I know that at times I was mean to my family, in particular my brother. We fought a lot during this time, and I think I was taking my anger out on him. I would make fun of him for his weight. He never did anything to deserve it. If anything, I was the fat and lazy one. (Metabolisms could start wars, I swear.)

There's a saying that I think holds true: Hurt people hurt people. Part of me was turning into a bully myself, at least when it came in between me being spoiled with something I thought the world owed me. I wanted to prove that I was better than everyone else, especially the people who made it a habit to remind me and others, verbatim, that they were "better than everyone else." Maybe then, people would see I was it — that I was somebody. Isn't that what we're all after?

CHAPTER 3
Turning the Page?

I was excited and nervous to start high school. I hoped it would be a new start — a chance to escape from the nightmare that was middle school. I decided that I wanted to play a sport in high school, so back in the 8th grade, my uncle Dan started teaching me how to play golf. I knew I wasn't in shape, and I wanted to change that. All throughout high school, the kids in my smaller hometown like my friends Alex, Drew, DJ, and Ben always played backyard games after school. I played football and basketball, often with guys who actually played these sports for the school, but I was too insecure to ever give it a chance. I was too insecure to learn how to play for real, so I chose golf.

At this point in my life, I had become incredibly shy in addition to being insecure. I was a very scrawny kid, and I was constantly insecure about not having a good enough body or looking cool enough. (I've always been a simple shirt and jeans guy.) When I joined the golf team, it allowed me to meet a lot of upperclassmen, and while I loved that, I still had a hard time opening up and connecting with people. As a freshman, I helped start a school newspaper with all upperclassmen. I loved it, but it was so hard to really be myself around these people. I wonder how many times we just take what people give us, unaware that like an iceberg, there is more below the surface. I know I've done it with others, and I wonder how many people have done this and believed so much less about me. Why do we live a story different than the one we want to live?

My first golf season went well. By went well, I mean we were terrible. Even so, I played every day. We were predominantly a team of freshmen, so I lettered my freshmen season. This was exciting to me because I believed, naturally, that we had a lot of potential to develop over the course of four years. I was also excited because I hoped the team would grow into a cohesive family. I was excited about the prospect of being an "athlete" and how it helped my image. I would have strangers ask me about the season, and it really helped me to make a few friends. Suddenly, I was more accepted by the jocks in my own grade. I think this was part of just growing up, but suddenly I was being befriended by the athletes in my grade. I was being invited to parties. Everything still wasn't perfect. I was still not a true local, which meant that I would always be kind of an outsider. I would still be the brunt of jokes, but things felt a little gentler now. Maybe things were turning around!

I developed a good friendship with a football guy named Spenser. I hated him in middle school. He was one of the reasons I quit football; he didn't like me. In ninth grade, we shared an English class, and we ended up bonding over an incredibly similar taste in ridiculous humor — Will Ferrell movies, Chuck Norris jokes, and pranks of all sorts. Spenser's favorite prank was to take off running and surprise me by tackling me into my locker. Twisted, but I thought it was hilarious. Later, Spenser ended up becoming my college roommate (where our affinity for pranks continued), and I'm still close with him and his family.

I had a couple of other friends, James and Andrew, who had been going to this youth group at a church near my house. They really liked it, and I noticed they had changed a lot since going. I had been to this church before and had tried a couple different things there, but never really felt a need to go regularly. James and Andrew were friends of mine from middle school, and they really wanted me to come. They're both influential guys. Both had charismatic, outrageous personalities. I tried things out in 8th grade, but high school was when I started going weekly. The youth pastor, Pastor Carl, was a cool guy, and the environment was fun. (They had video games, come on!) Some people would play music, and Pastor Carl would talk about Jesus. A lot of the elementary kids I grew up with went there, so it became a social event for me. I wasn't so sure about the church building or the idea of religion. Sure, I thought there is probably a God, but it seemed so antique to me. Religion was a relic in my mind and so were the wacky people that follow it. Youth group was enticing enough still, and soon it was a normal part of my week. I really felt like I could be myself there.

During the winter of my freshmen year, James and Andrew had this idea. We were all diehard pro wrestling fans. We would wrestle on couches in Andrew's basement or order the WWE pay-per-views. This was around the time where YouTube had exploded in popularity. We started to discover these crazy videos of kids wrestling in their backyards and building their own rings, all to make these internet films. We knew we wanted to do that. We secured all the supplies — tires, wood, carpet and tarps to build a wrestling base — and then we recruited a kid to film and edit, set up some speakers for intro music, and proceeded to film ourselves wrestling weekly — snow, rain, or shine. Several friends like Ben, Kevin, and more joined in. We'd create characters, storylines, had championship belts, and slam each other for hours. And so, KPW was born. The whole experience was like crazy creative euphoria! We would add videos to YouTube and even burn DVDs to give to people in school. It was a smash hit! We had created a subculture. By May, we held a live event and had well over 100 kids there to watch. My life fortunes were looking up. Positive things were happening. I was building relationships with more "important" peers. I was being praised for a lot in my life. I was going to church, so that made me a "good kid." Most importantly, girls(!) were talking to me! I was an athlete and living the wrestling dream. (I even "won" the KPW title.) All the pain from the past was seemingly gone. School was still awkward, but things were looking up. Maybe I could do anything I set my mind to.

The Fall

(Playlist songs 6)

In May 2006, my grandmother Ruth passed away. She had fought a long battle with diabetes and succumbed to natural causes. I mentioned earlier that my grandmother was the sweetest person I had ever met. There weren't many things (or people) that made me feel valued. The care I received from her was rare. I recognize that many people won't share this type of bond with any family members, let alone grandparents. My heart breaks for those people. This made her passing all the more difficult. It exposed me to the reality of death. Something good was gone, and I would never have it back in this life. Death affected my life, if anything, by magnifying the things I was desiring.

Who wants to die a failure?

This was a catalyst event that also seemed to begin a never-ending cycle of stress for my family. It didn't matter what — health, finances, drama, decisions — it always seemed to be one thing after another for my whole family. That, or I was becoming more aware of the realities of life.

Regardless, I went into the summer high on life. I began feeling some of the freedoms of being a teenager. I think I saw every movie that came out in theaters that summer. I even had a few short relationships! They didn't last, but what lasts at that age? I spent most of my time swimming, watching wrestling, and wasting time on the internet. I played enough golf to remember which way to swing the club, as they say. When school came back around, I had the highest of hopes. I was going to be great at golf and maybe join other sports, see what could happen with girls, and take my rightful place with the "cool" kids.

Almost immediately, golf got off to a bad start. My teammates had worked all winter, spring, and summer to improve, and it showed. I had maintained my existing skills. I kept a starting spot, but I was significantly worse compared to others. The season proved to be a real strain, as I grew more defeated and distressed by my level of play. I was not close friends with my teammates; I think they put up with me rather than trying to include me. We all just had different interests. Our team finished second in our section, which I believe in large part was due to me being a weak link. It didn't help that one of my female teammates won her first of two individual state championships that season. (She is now an LPGA professional.) I felt like a disappointment.

School itself proved to be a challenge. Classes were harder, and I wasn't too motivated to really work hard. I was becoming more exposed to the world out there and learning about societal issues. I was learning that the world was a scary, dangerous, and unforgiving place. More than ever, I needed friends to help me feel comfortable and confident. At first, friendships started off all right socially, but eventually, they began to regress. I was again a popular target for mockery. High school was a competitive place, and I slipped back into feeling like I couldn't measure up. I know a lot of kids experience something like my this in school. Most days, I would walk into school, down the hallways and the lobby, and would feel invisible. People had their circles to walk in; meanwhile, I'd wander around the cold brick and locker lined hallways wondering if anyone cared. Most of my peers had developed friendships with older students and their teammates, but many of my friends either were too busy for me or were just naturally growing more distant.

It was becoming evident that in the social ladder of life, I had friends who were cutting me from their teams. Myspace was the biggest social media site in the world at the time, and it had this feature where you could include your best friends in a "Top 8." I know this caused wars somewhere. As an emotional wreck of a fifteen-year-old, I let removal from these lists go to my head. *I guess I'm expendable?* I can remember being rude and condescending to a few friends during this time. Think of the scene in the movie *Mean Girls* where Lindsay Lohan inadvertently hurts her real friends while dealing with drama with the cool kids. Basically, that was my life at this point.

I was falling into a pattern of expecting disappointment. I had a few ugly rejections from girls that really hurt my self-worth. I started failing in outlets like KPW and golf. I was either being abandoned by friends or treated as worthless by others. I began to do poorly in school. I hadn't needed to study before that point, and I assumed that things would work themselves out. My parents demanded that I do my very best and work hard. This expectation wasn't to the extremes we sometimes see in society, but there were expectations and the pressure that comes with them nonetheless. I began to question the point of it all. I lived in a pretty middle class/impoverished area. Our community seemed to glorify mediocrity. Many of my peers (certainly not all) were sacrificing things they were interested in and buying into cookie-cutter career plans such as being lawyers, accountants, or doctors. *Okay, good for you, but what's the point? Why go through any of that if you aren't happy?*

Numb

(Playlist songs 7 & 8)

The pain was often suffocating. I felt invisible to most. In the region where I lived, it stays very cold from about late October through March. It's a consistently cloudy area, so add some leafless trees, and you get a pretty gloomy environment — the kind of environment where a miserable kid would stare out the window of a long bus ride every day wondering if suffering and decay is all we're served. I know that I wasn't the only one. I had peers go through serious family issues as well — poverty, divorce, tragedy. There was a popular girl at school who sadly passed away in a car crash that rocked our community. I remember feeling sad for the tragedy itself, but also for myself because I was becoming so used to the hurt. It would hurt me to see other people being hurt at school, but I felt powerless to help. This was also around the time of the Virginia Tech Massacre, and in a class, we were studying the Columbine tragedy extensively. I was overwhelmed with the constant reminders we live in a painful, horrific world.

Again, I felt powerless to address the issues I saw. I had empathy for kids with physical and mental disabilities as well as those without friends. I'd try to befriend these people and do things like sit by them at lunch. I would get ridiculed for this. I knew what they were feeling. It would make me sick to see them openly mocked. I never did anything to confront people over this cruelty, I didn't even stand up for myself usually. I wish I had been more intentional at friendships with these types of students in middle and high school. That's a regret for sure, and it only added to the pain I felt.

During that school year, I became emotionally numb. I think it was a psychological defense mechanism. Sometimes the pain would be too much to keep down, and I would cry myself to sleep. I stopped taking care of myself physically during this time. I gained a lot of weight during these months and grew long hair. I remember that winter, I went with my family to see the Ben Stiller movie, *Night at the Museum*. Fine. Family friendly movie, I get it, but what was so strange and bizarre was that I cried at the end of the film. It's a happy ending, and I felt happy after seeing it. I had not felt an intense emotion for months, so I was moved to tears because I could still *feel* something. Sadly, it didn't last long, I soon went back to feeling numb. I felt like an exile, someone who didn't belong anywhere.

I still never opened up to anyone during this time. I had a friend named Adam. Adam is one of the most intelligent and eclectic guys I've ever met, and now he's off dominating graduate programs in Japanese and Asian studies and traveling the globe. He was sensitive to the fact that things weren't right in my life and was a consistent encouragement to me. He helped me see writing as a creative and emotional outlet. I've never forgotten those people and moments that helped me to find the courage to keep going. There's no possible way they know the depths of how they helped me.

I don't know when suicide first became something I consciously thought about. I had known peers who had mental health issues. The last thing I wanted was to be on medicine and see a psychologist. Ironically, I was listening to music and seeing movies that had suicide references around this time, and I think it fed this idea. I had this sense that nothing would ever change. Life was always going to be mediocre and hopeless. I didn't want to actually hurt myself. I knew that was crazy, and I knew I needed non-judgmental help. It was a hard impulse to overcome though. One night I was overwhelmed, crying, and I sat in my kitchen staring at a knife. *Is this what it is going to come to?* I remembered a story, real or not, that someone I knew wanted to kill themselves, but the gun jammed when they pulled the trigger. This person had sensed that God had a plan for their life, that they weren't alone, and their life was spared. I thought maybe I should read the Bible. I hadn't given that much thought, and I thought the things talked about at youth group were nice, so what's to lose? I was able to go to bed.

CHAPTER 4
Jesus

(Playlist songs 9 – 12)

Just after Spring break of my sophomore year, my family went on a vacation to Playa Del Carmen, just south of Cancun. To me, the idea of going on this trip was a waste of time. I was doing poorly in school, and I did not have the motivation to do much of anything. School felt like prison. Every day gave me more reasons to think I couldn't measure up, and people did not care. Most days, I felt a cloud over me. There was a sense of impending doom over me. My fears about life would find me. I wasn't ever going to be good enough. Maybe I was going to die young. The aesthetic of my life was decay. (Wow, that sounds so emo.) I didn't have healthy relationships with peers, lived in an area that I think would have been best described as forgotten, and found most of my joy in being a spectator to everything. Could anything ever change? Not much pointed me to thinking it could. So, what was the point in going on vacation?

My family had never been big into vacations when I was young. When I was early elementary age, we took a couple Disney vacations, but by middle and high school, the go-to vacation was camping. It took at least half a year for my mother and I to get our passports back after applying. They came in the mail the day before we left for Mexico. I thought maybe that meant I was in for a memorable experience. I had no idea.

I love flying. I love airports. Everything about the experience is cool to me. Sure, sometimes the lines and hurrying is annoying, but I love people-watching, and airports feel like melting pots of the world. Literally going somewhere helps you feel better about where your life is going, too.

We flew to Mexico and arrived at our resort. I was happy to be away from everything going on in my life. The weather was hot, and so it was a great reprieve from the still freezing Pennsylvania spring. The resort was cool. Not every employee spoke English, and guests from all over the world stayed there, too. I appreciated getting to see the local markets and experience a different culture. The beach stood out the most for me. I had never seen water so blue. I couldn't believe something like this could exist. I was privileged to go snorkeling and was in awe of the thousands of fish and all the colors one could see. Again, I couldn't believe any of this was real.

One night after dinner, I decided I wanted to walk down to the beach. The moon and stars were out, and the light reflected off the water and lit up the sand, all while the warm, salty air felt calming. I stayed there awhile. It was one of the most gorgeous sights I had ever seen. Sometimes in life, you get hit with moments that feel too good to be true, and this was one. I thought the daylight proved unbelievable, but this was even better. I remember being overwhelmed with emotions. I felt like everything was going to be all right.

In that moment, it felt like God was talking to me. I know how that sounds, but I don't mean in an audible way. I sensed in that moment that it was as if God was telling me, "Look at what I've created. None of this is by accident. I created this and everything to be enjoyed. Not only did I care enough to create this, but your life is no accident either. Life is supposed to be so much more. I love you. Will you walk with me and let me show you what life can be? Can I show you what it means to love and follow me?"

I had been reading the Bible for a few months and had been learning about Jesus and what He did. I didn't hear any voice speaking to me, but what I was experiencing that night was too real to be denied. I knew just from reading the scriptures that following Jesus didn't make life easier or without pain, but I knew that I needed better. I knew I was carrying pain, and I knew I had sin (you could think of it as destructive issues) in my life. That night, I decided to start a relationship with Jesus.

Tabula Rasa

One of my favorite books of the Bible is Galatians. The Apostle Paul, who wrote a large part of the New Testament, wrote this letter to the church in the ancient city of Galatia, now modern-day Turkey. Some Jewish extremists were trying to convince non-Jewish Christians that they had to follow certain Jewish rituals to gain salvation, regardless of faith. They had to "earn it."

Apparently, time doesn't change many things. I think it is normal in today's world for people to feel like they must live up to expectations to belong...like we have to make up for all the ways we fail to earn forgiveness, to feel blameless... like people have to conform to someone else's image to have a good life. This is what was at issue in the Galatian church. The "outsiders," those who "didn't belong," had to work to earn God's love. Paul throws all that out.

Paul writes in Galatians that in God's eyes, it doesn't matter if you are a Jew or not. He writes that salvation has nothing to do with what you do, but that it comes from grace by faith in what Jesus has done (vs. 16). He goes on to say that if we could live up to God's law on our own, then Christ died for nothing (vs. 21). Paul writes that because of Jesus' death and resurrection, we can have a new life and forgiveness of sins. Galatians 2:20 says, "I have been crucified with Christ, and I no longer live, but Christ lives in me. The life I now live in the body, I live by faith in the Son of God, who loved me and gave himself for me."

This reminds me of a philosophical concept called Tabula Rasa, which is a Latin phrase that can be translated as meaning "blank slate." The concept is that children are born into the world with no knowledge about the world or how it works. Everything is new. Not that this is a Biblical concept, but a "blank slate" is what I experienced after I decided to begin a relationship with Jesus. I had a renewed sense of wonder. Scripture says that the Holy Spirit comes in to your life at salvation. It was as if the Holy Spirit was telling me, "Everything can be different now; everything you've experienced doesn't have to define you anymore. You can actually live a new life through Me."

Everything Began to Change

(Playlist songs 13-15)

I wanted to do everything I could to learn more about Jesus. I got back home and decided I wanted to read the Bible, so I started with the New Testament to learn about Him. I was ignorant of most Biblical stories and even the larger narrative, but I knew that I had accepted Jesus and needed to know Him. I had been taught that much. I read about how Jesus loved the forgotten and unforgivable. He didn't play games with politicians, religious legalists/hypocrites or social posturers. His message of the Beatitudes is recorded in Matthew 5 saying things like, "Blessed are the poor in spirit, those who mourn, the merciful, pure in heart, those persecuted for righteousness," and more. Safe to say, Matthew 5 is worth reading. Throughout it, Jesus teaches about His Father and how the Kingdom of God is different and better than anything we know.

Youth group became more serious to me. There were weeks when getting to Wednesday night became my refuge. I was living on a Jesus high. I started going to youth retreats and conferences. Things weren't always easy. Life circumstances didn't necessarily get any better. I still had bad days. Jesus was awesome and gave me hope, but was He actually there when life got hard? Was I just creating an imaginary friend?

That summer, before my junior year of high school, my family took a trip out to visit my aunt and uncle who lived in the Salt Lake Valley in Utah. I had never been that far west before, and I was amazed at how much it felt like a different world. I had never seen skies so clear and blue. I thought I knew what mountains were, but nothing compared to the magnitude of these giant limestone and dolomite formations. We visited in July, and there was still snow cap on the mountains. I love hot weather. Dry heat is a gift from God — I'm convinced.

My uncle Bill took us to many different locations in the valley. We got to go clay shooting at the state shooting club. We traveled through the desert to see the San Rafael Swell (Utah's Little Grand Canyon). Being out in a desert full of mountains, I couldn't shake the feeling that this was God's country. Everything was so expansive and peaceful. We saw pictographs on rocks that were thousands of years old. We explored Salt Lake City and learned about the Mormon religion, even visiting the location of the temple. (You can't go in if you aren't Mormon.) I'm grateful to have experienced many things in Utah, thankfully having returned a few times since, but one thing always sticks out.

July 3, 2007, is a day I will never forget. This was supposed to be a guys' day out while all the females went shopping. So, my uncle, grandpa, brother, and I set out after an adventure early that morning. We drove up to a trail in Provo. My brother and I climbed up a waterfall on the side of a mountain at the end of the trail. Following that, we drove to Sundance Mountain Resort and rode the ski lift. It was breathtaking. On our way back to our next adventure, there was an accident along Route 189 right in front of us. The whole highway was shut down, so we got out and ate our packed lunches sitting down on the highway. It truly was a bizarre and unique experience.

Next, we had signed up to go on a tubing trip down the Provo River. My uncle had heard it was a great time. There were rafting options, but we were told it was calm enough to be in individual tubes. We got down to the river as other tubers and rafters were setting off. So far, so good. Sure, things looked a little shady — but, hey, whatever.

As each of us guys set off, it was instantly difficult to steer the tube. I was a scrawny fifteen-year old; I could barely reach over to steer, bouncing from one edge of the river to another, scraping along branches and rocks. My twelve-year old brother Alan and my seventy-nine-year old grandpa were having a good deal of trouble themselves. Soon, my grandpa and I started to get the hang of it, and my uncle stayed back to help my brother. We were given a couple instructions on the lengthy ride. A few times, we would come to a Y in the river where it bent around some land and were instructed to stay to the left. At the first Y, we were close enough that with one hand I grabbed my grandfather's tube and with the other grabbed onto the back of a raft and let it gently take us around the Y. The people in the raft then discovered us and poked at me with oars to let go. (Could they not see the seventy-nine-year old?) As we continued, the river seemed to really ease up, and Grandpa and I coasted along. I even got to talk with a couple other tubers as the river took us. At one point, I started talking with a girl a few years older than me, and she gave me some tips on how to navigate the Y we were approaching. My grandpa had lagged behind, falling out of sight, so I followed the girl around the Y.

Once I was around land, the river straightened out, and I decided to hold course until my grandpa caught up. After about a minute I noticed a raft floating down river upside-down from the right side of the little island. Instantly, my heart started pounding. I jumped out of my tube. I feared it was my grandpa, and I had to act fast. The water was chest deep, most of it melted snow from the Wasatch Mountains, all of it a freezing forty degrees. Wading along with the current, I grabbed the tube and found my grandpa somehow hanging on underneath. He was barely conscious. I didn't have the slightest clue what to do.

I wasn't sure if I should let go of my tube to gain better balance or if holding onto the top was keeping us afloat. I tried my best to get my footing, but I kept flailing against the current and the river floor. I was being dragged under the water every few seconds, and I was doing my best to keep Grandpa above the water. I wasn't sure if he was still conscious or not, but he was holding his tube still. I remember I kept screaming out, "Please, God!" and "Help!" After what seemed like forever, we landed on a side of the river where it was shallower, and I walked us to the edge. I have no idea how, but I was able to flip Grandpa's tube, and with one arm, lift him into his tube. Not a minute later, two other guys floated down and helped me get our tubes and Grandpa out of the water. Thankfully, I had some water in my tube that Grandpa, who was barely hanging on, was able to sip on and recover. Within minutes, my uncle and brother showed up, and the two men left for help. Soon, a rescue team arrived, and we all waded back across to safety.

We got back to the house and recouped with the rest of the family. Grandpa was doing much better and just needed to rest. As if we hadn't had enough adventure for one day, we had plans lined up already to go free climbing and repelling that night with a guide. Despite everything, we decided to go anyway and went back out to the desert. We stopped at a rock cliff a couple hundred feet tall. We took our time, gradually climbing up the side and finally made it to the top. Our plan at the top was to repel halfway down to a ledge and reposition.

I found repelling for the first time to be an incredibly difficult experience. On my first descent, I slipped and went smashing into some sagebrush on the rock face. Later, after we all got down the ledge, we discovered that something wasn't quite right with my harness. Our guide assured me after everyone descended that he would come back around and bring what I needed to get down. This was about seven o'clock in the evening. At nine-thirty, it was dark, and I was still sitting on this ledge. The guide had become lost trying to get back around to find our cliff. Eventually, he found us and climbed down to me. He explained that it was too dark and we needed to climb back up. I used hand clamps and climbed back up the rock, before climbing down the side.

It was after midnight by the time I crawled into bed that night. I was stunned by all I had seen and the potentially life-threatening experiences I had just gone through. I couldn't help but feel grateful and believe that God had protected me throughout the day. Now I'm not insinuating that God is a genie or that He always protects us from bad things happening. In my view, that perspective is not biblical. What I really do think is that God was teaching me that day how He is present amid crazy and scary situations. We never go through anything alone, and I believe He protected us that day. I choose to think He used this experience to teach me about who He is.

Growing

(Playlist song 16)

Going into my junior year, I particularly wrestled with understanding how to live out my faith. A lot of my insecurities did not go away. I was still chasing after girls I knew I shouldn't. I was like Cameron in the movie *Ferris Bueller's Day Off*. I had built up the idea of girls and physical intimacy as the be-all and end-all despite everything I was learning about Jesus. This proved to be an issue that would haunt me later. However, as Ferris would say, I was learning that "life moves fast, and I needed to look around once in a while."

What became an issue is that I felt like I was supposed to talk about my faith, but I wasn't sure how. I'd try inviting friends to church, but most would say they'd think about it and never commit. Sometimes, it was hard to avoid feeling discouraged. I had some outlets that helped me get through. I was developing more of a passion for music. I found some bands that sang about Jesus that weren't too bad. I started learning how to play guitar, but I'd get discouraged by how hard it was. Still, I found it to be fun. I had a group of friends that I spent a lot of time playing basketball with, watching sports, and going to the movies. It was little things like this that I valued. Youth group became a weekly refuge where I was encouraged in my faith, even when it was hard to understand some of the harsh realities of life.

I remember hearing a Jeremy Camp song taken from 2 Corinthians 5:7, which says we walk by faith and not by sight. This became an idea that helped shape my understanding of faith. Just because I had become a Christian did not mean that everything made sense, and it didn't mean that I did not struggle with issues. I remember worrying that my struggles with depression would come back. Some days, when I would feel discouraged or alone, I would almost feel myself creeping back into a haze. I still compared myself to others. I began to wonder what I was supposed to do with my life. Many of my friends and peers at school still made me feel insignificant. Sometimes, I'd be intentionally left out of friend's plans or conversations. I would not have necessarily been able to verbalize it at the time, but I knew I wanted to accomplish things and feel worth it to the people I wanted approval from. I had friends who had all sorts of qualities that made them significant — friends that were great athletes, successful at school, wealthy, had relationships, or had incredible talents. At times, I felt like I had none of these things and wasn't exactly sure what I wanted to do with my life as my senior year approached. And what did faith have to do with any of that? As my junior year was ending, I had more questions than answers, but I clung to the idea I had to walk by faith.

During this time, I felt like God was teaching me a lot about creativity and living with a sense of passion. My friends had outrageous personalities, and it rubbed off on me. I also feel like I learned something about spirituality. As I learned more about the Gospel, I felt that we aren't meant to live like life is lackluster or not worth it. Jesus is quoted in John 10:10 (KJV) saying, "I have come that you may have life more abundant." I think that is a verse that some people have misinterpreted for selfish pursuits, but what I learned in this season was that maybe life was meant to be enjoyed and lived fully. I became involved helping make TV productions at school, and my friends and I made home videos of all sorts. We combined our passion for film with wrestling, music, and movies. We lived in a place where there wasn't much culture to take in, so we went about creating culture. This naturally seeped into how I saw faith; when you follow Jesus, you are more alive.

I noticed changes in my life that following summer. I've established that my friends and I were outrageous and had twisted humor. We would do dumb things. Dumb things like wait for it to snow a lot and then go spin out our cars. Sometimes we would prank call random numbers and say totally inappropriate things. (We were raised on a healthy diet of Dave Chappelle, *South Park*, and WWE after all.) One time, we pranked someone we knew and went really, really, too far. Long story short, the police were called, and we quickly owned up to it before things got crazier. We individually had our pastors come to our houses and talk with us. It was quite embarrassing, and I was confronted with the reality that I had done something ugly. Here I was calling myself a follower of Jesus, and I blatantly hurt people.

The summer proved to be an important time of reflection for me. For some reason, I've always been a big legacy person. Maybe I was buying into the clichés, but I was excited for my senior year, to be toward my future. I mainly golfed and listened to music all summer. It gave me a lot of time to think about what

I wanted to do. Maybe I wanted to keep working on editing videos or go into journalism. (I was the high school's paper editor.) I heard nurses had great job outlook and made great money. I dreamed of playing guitar for a living. Many of my friends were feeling called to church ministry, but I didn't feel special enough to do that, and besides, I wanted to make money. What did it mean to be called or hear God's voice? I think I thought about every single major I could find, and I struggled throughout my senior year with anxiety over it. The last thing I wanted was to do something that didn't feel true to me.

I distinctly remember being a prospective student at engineering camp when I was thinking about heaven of all things. *What really is my end goal? Could I be missing out on a better life God wants for me?* I began to ask myself these questions, and while I didn't have many answers, things began to stir in me. I began to feel conviction that my life needed to be different if I followed Jesus. Maybe I should really watch the things I say, treat people better, and not be so selfish. Around this time, I had become sexually active, and I would feel a lot of guilt. Some of this came from toxic relationships pressuring me, and some came from my selfishness leading me to it. Deep down, I knew better, and I wanted to be better. I felt these convictions to be different, not because I felt like I needed to live up to any rules, but because I was experiencing better with Jesus, and I believed ultimately, that He wants better for us.

I think this is what Jesus is getting at in the interactions we see in the Gospels. For example, in John 8, Jesus speaks to a woman caught in adultery. He doesn't condemn her. She knows what she has done is wrong. He tells her to go, and sin no more. Jesus isn't saying to her, "You have to do this on your own to earn my love and forgiveness." He is saying that he wants to heal her, and show her better. He hasn't come to judge her, but He doesn't sugarcoat things either. He wants better for her, and he wants better for all of us. We see in the Gospels that Jesus is about the Kingdom. Jesus came for atonement; He came so we can be reconciled to Him — the only way to true satisfaction. I was slowly, not perfectly, learning this about my life, actions, and goals. *Maybe I should be living for more?*

Who Should I Be?

(Playlist song 17)

There's an amazing quote from CS Lewis that I love. He is quoted as saying:

> "It would seem that Our Lord finds our desires not too strong, but too weak. We are half-hearted creatures, fooling about with drink and sex and ambition when infinite joy is offered us, like an ignorant child who wants to go on making mud pies in a slum because he cannot imagine what is meant by the offer of a holiday at the sea. We are far too easily pleased."

I remember hearing that quote and having my mind blown. It certainly resonated with the life I was experiencing. I've established that I certainly wasn't immune to temptations, but I observed many peers living up to different identities. Everyone commits his or her life to something. Some people would say we all "worship" something. We all decide what is most important to us. We all know what our heart desires most. Many peers were deciding to live up to the cultural norms around us. You have to decide what you're going to live for. Is it athletics or academics? Is it partying or cynicism? What are your political views? At the time (and still), I didn't think badly about things like sports, jobs, or other commitments, but I couldn't help but feel like people were putting their eggs all in one basket that wouldn't ultimately satisfy. It was hard to articulate what I was thinking.

When you're a baby Christian, sometimes all you understand is that Jesus loves you and offers better. *Well, what exactly is better?* That's a common thing nonbelievers will struggle with — they just don't see the point. In this time, I was beginning to have the sense that following Jesus did lead to a better life and hope of an afterlife. Later, I would read a book called *Unfashionable* by Tullian Tchvidjian that helped me understand this idea better. Following Jesus is about being different because our hope is in a kingdom and a way of life so radically different than our own. Jesus defines success and fulfillment in different terms than we would. I wish I would have understood this better at the time.

Sometimes, I wondered if I was missing it. I had days where I wouldn't feel anything at all. For as much as I had experienced cool things and had reasons to believe in Jesus, I would also have days where I would feel alone. I had days where I questioned if God was actually there. Following Jesus proved to be exhausting at times. I had friends who lived like faith was such a natural way of doing life, but I often felt like an imposter trying to fit in. I carried a lot of guilt over knowing I still had so many issues. I still wanted to do a lot of things I knew I shouldn't. I had read verses about how God would make you a new creation, and I had a hard time believing it. *Am I really saved? Maybe I'm not as special or worthy enough to be a Christian. Maybe I don't really know God. Am I too bad to be forgiven? Why do I feel like I'm in the dark when I'm trying to follow Him?*

I carried many of these frustrations into a trip in August. My youth group took a large group to a national youth conference in Charlotte, NC (gorgeous area). We ended up staying in a campground in all wooden cabins. What ensued was complete shenanigans as my friends and I terrorized our chaperones and peers through pranks, making a giant mess, and other totally intelligent ideas like going streaking in the early hours of the morning. We also did the normal stuff: Acting like fools in public, such as starting a chanting "human train" in the convention center before sessions.

Something changed in me over the course of this trip. It is rather difficult to explain. Overall, it was an amazing conference with great speakers and music, but the themes were about passion and desperation. I didn't want to have a lackluster faith that made no difference in my life or others. I wanted to be moved to compassion; I didn't want to be selfish or indifferent. One night at the conference, there was an extended time of music and an opportunity for students to come down and pray (simply talk to God) on the arena floor to know the Holy Spirit more. Things like this made me uncomfortable because I didn't want to draw unwanted attention to myself or just do something to look spiritual. I decided to go pray anyway because I had felt moved. I remember praying specifically for all my friends at school. I prayed my faith wouldn't be about trying to live up to anyone else's ideas. I wanted a vibrant relationship that infused every part of my life. I remember praying until I just couldn't verbalize what I was thinking anymore, but I kept praying out loud in words I didn't know. Pentecostal preachers tend to speak to experiences like this. Honestly, it was weird, but all I know is I felt so focused on these things, and an overwhelming sense of peace came over me. It was one of those moments where God felt so close, and I knew I was experiencing a new intimacy with Him. I left that conference feeling more alive, knowing God loved me, and knowing I had a mission to share that love with my peers.

My senior year provided some challenges. I remember thinking it was the biggest year of my life. I wanted to finally see healing in relationships, but I also couldn't wait to get out of town. My senior golf season was poised for great things. I was entrenched as a normal starter by this time, had better camaraderie with my teammates than years past, and was playing some of the best rounds of my life. I had dated a few different girls around this time. I was going to be successful in school and find the perfect college choice for me. I was dedicated to being a "Christian example," meaning I wanted everyone to think highly of me and bring people to church. I would soon learn this was more about my ego than I realized. This year taught me a lot about pain.

I realized how wrapped up in myself I had become. It took a lot of pain to see this. I peaked about midway through my senior golf season, then declined from fatigue, weather, and stress. I never golfed under par again. It was still another championship season for my team, but another disappointment for me individually while my teammates progressed and excluded me from celebrations. *Am I always going to be a disappointment?* This year showed me my peers were moving further into the identities they were wanting to live out, and simply trying to have faith conversations with them received a lot of pushback. I didn't know any better but to take this personally. One relationship my senior year significantly affected me.

It was simply toxic. We fed each other's egos and shortcomings. Probably still the worst aspect of this relationship was the emotional rollercoaster. Some days, we were very hot. Other days, we were very cold. Sometimes we helped each other feel like the most incredible person alive, but other days, we would bitterly tear each other down. Add in all the mess of unhealthy intimacy, and this toxic relationship had wrecked me personally. By the time the relationship ended, I felt like I had lost my future. I dreamed of being with this girl; she knew me as well as anyone. How do you move forward when you put all your eggs in one basket, and then that basket falls apart? I knew this relationship was toxic to my developing faith and it left me having to figure out if it made sense to keep trying to anchor my life around faith moving forward.

As I was struggling personally, this year also helped me to see more clearly how hateful we can be to each other. Maybe it was because I was trying to learn more about how to care for people, but I remember feeling so heartbroken about many things. I had always hated how my peers, who maybe came from less than privileged backgrounds, would be called "grubs."

Why can't we just treat each other as human beings? I was in my senior English class (I was too lazy to take the college level class), and I was mocked for tutoring a peer. I had grown up in elementary school with him, and I wanted to help him pass so he could graduate.

I have never forgotten those people. Maybe it is wanting to fix the past, but I still dream of ways to go give back to the communities and people who loved me. *Why can't we look beyond ourselves and help each other live better lives?* I had many peers who made fun of other students with mental and physical disabilities and the very backward and isolated. I hate to admit that it was so easy to do nothing. It was so easy to awkwardly laugh along and not confront people. At times I would, but nobody cared. I tried befriending these students the best I knew how, but sometimes I felt helpless.

I cared because so many times I had felt the same way they did. Sometimes, people would be so guarded that kind words would go in one ear and out the other. My area growing up wasn't incredibly diverse, so I was shielded from many of the issues of racism. I had plenty of friends from different ethnicities and wouldn't learn until later many of the horrors of racism that still exist. One of my favorite movies to watch around this time was the movie *Boyz 'n the Hood.* While certainly not an expert, I felt this film opened my eyes to some of the issues facing minorities. It depicts some of the challenges of living in poverty, the challenges of being mistreated just because of your skin color. It helped me to be more conscious of things I'm ignorant of. It made me want to pay attention to different types of music, films, and voices.

I can honestly say this was a dark time for me. It had been a couple years since I had found new hope and decided to follow Jesus. I was facing a lot of uncertainty. *Is this hope real?* Winter still found me feeling isolated and afraid. A college decision was coming down to the wire, and I had more questions than any sense of direction. Friends were conveniently leaving me out of trips, parties, and life plans. *Has anyone ever really cared about me this whole time? Where is God in all of this? That girl told me I wasn't good enough…and maybe it's true. Am I meant to think life is a tease?*

What I was going through is normal for most high school seniors. You have known life one way, and it's hard to comprehend that anything can be around the corner you can't see. This is a microcosm of life and faith. It is easy to tell people you should believe there are good things around the corner or there's meaning to what you are going through, but it can be so difficult to believe when you are living it. My insecurities were running wild again. I felt like my life was ending. *What's the point of going to college, of having a job if pain is all it ends in? I've lived it up as a kid with no responsibilities, but now everything is crashing. Where is my hope?*

I remember this all came to a head in the spring. One day my friends and I thought it would be a good idea to put on MMA gloves and legitimately casually fight each other (as in, just don't kill each other). My younger, physically massive brother challenged me, and after three rounds of five minutes, we were exhausted. (To this day we dispute who won, but I saw stars and went black for a few moments enduring some ground and pound.)

Once we were back resting in my friend Andrew's basement, I broke down into uncontrollable sobbing. I realized I was just physically fighting my only brother and became appalled. The weight of carrying so much hurt for myself and others was suffocating. My friends cared for me and prayed for me. That's all I ever wanted was to matter and feel cared for. Isn't that what we all want? My friends assured me we would always be there for each other.

Ephesians 4:2 is a passage of scripture that really stuck with me in this time. It reads, "Be completely humble and gentle; be patient, bearing with one another in love." The more I was studying and reading, I was learning this is an important command in following Jesus. A few verses later it speaks to "unity" of "peace" with each other as we cling to "one hope" of faith in Jesus. I was learning that following Jesus meant we needed to bear each other's burdens. My friends were important to me and had power to impact my life. The truth is, we all have this opportunity. If faith was to be real in my life, I needed to care for people. James chapter 2 in scripture affirms this.

I had been carrying so much pain and learned that we see hope come to life when we care for each other. Realizing this led to a lot of changes in my life. I wanted to do something about all the hurt I was seeing. I started asking people for forgiveness in regard to times I had been so selfish. I believe this started a chain of mental dominoes leading me to choose Psychology as my college major. I figured helping people was what I was meant to naturally do.

Perhaps my greatest takeaway from high school was the importance of shenanigans. It's a conviction of mine that life isn't meant to be stale. Being all neat and proper is great but hardly gives life or influence. I'm thankful I had outrageous friends who pushed me to dream, regardless how out of touch with reality we sometimes were. In any given day at school, I knew anything ridiculous could be around the corner. Somehow, we could do most anything we wanted. Whether that was one of us leaving school for a midday Sheetz run or hanging out in the gym all day. I was the senior editor of the newspaper (Thank you, Kim!) and during school could work on it all I wanted. I was in a film club where my friends and I were constantly making SNL, MTV, and MadTv parodies as well as filming utter nonsense whenever we could. (Yeah, it was often wrestling.) Anytime it snowed, my friends and I would take our cars out to straight stretches and spin out. Playing video games together for days on end or staying up all night was normal. Hosting truck-stop breakfast sandwich (RIP Heavy Hauler) eating competitions was something totally normal to us. It was just fun knowing life didn't have to always be lived inside of lines someone else determined. This had a profound impact on the way I saw faith. Pursuing Jesus and sharing Him with people needed to be a little crazy and fun and risky because we live in a world that is a little crazy and fun and risky. Playing it safe makes an impact on no one.

I was eager to leave high school, but I was plenty nervous nonetheless. I had the hardest time imagining there could be anything left. I had lived almost eighteen years in the same place, with the same people, in the same environment. Regardless of how hard some things were, it was all I knew. The relationships with teachers and friends were important to me. I knew that I cared so much about what others thought of me, and I knew I made many decisions in my life based on how I believed others would perceive me. *"Will I get made fun of for this?"* is basically how I made choices. *How can there be a different chapter to life?* When you've always had the same friends, gone to the same places, it can be rather scary to imagine starting something new.

If you're reading this, and you're going through a scary transition period (like leaving high school), then know this: A lot of people will tell you that it will work out fine. Often, these are just lazy answers. Everyone's lives are different, and they play out differently. There's too much advice out there for me to get at it all for right now. What I can tell you (and what the rest of this book will get at) it is that it doesn't have to be scary. We aren't alone. Joy is possible always. No decision wrecks you forever. Let me explain my perspective.

I knew when leaving high school that I wanted to reset everything. I knew I wanted to go my own way in life. I wanted to break free from insecurities. I wanted to be in an environment where I could have peace of mind; I wanted to know that I wasn't going to be jumped and abused anytime a vulnerable moment came. I didn't want to feel the pressure of fitting in. I didn't want to be forced to live up to others' expectations anymore. I decided I wanted to go to a local private university. I also seriously considered West Virginia University and a Christian school in Florida. To me, it seemed like a comfortable choice. I wasn't super confident, but I had to choose something. I just couldn't figure out what it meant to "hear God's call."

Some Christians around me truly believed they knew what God wanted them to do. I felt completely in the dark and was desperate to know my place in the world. I'll never forget one comment which influenced me heavily: I told a buddy about my college choice, and they dropped an insult thinly disguised as humor, "Well, we never expected much out of you anyway."

Right before graduation, my aunt and some cousins took me to the Bahamas with them. Being back at a Caribbean beach like where I first had a strong encounter with God felt like a reminder from Him — He was still with me, and he would be in the future. This trip gave me another opportunity to realize how incredible life is. I got to swim with dolphins (A year later we'd come back and get to swim with sea lions!). It was hard to experience this and think life wasn't special. The trip also was a great opportunity to "people watch," too. I was getting older and thinking more about the type of person I should be as an adult. My senior year featured the high-profile first election of Barack Obama. I spent more time that year doing things like reading the newspaper and paying attention to what was going on around the country. I paid more attention to the needs people expressed. On this trip, it hit me — how can we waste so much time and so many resources? *Is happiness really making a lot of money so I can buy nice clothes and party at the casino?* I just couldn't help trying to shake the feeling that our lives are supposed to be more.

High school ended with celebratory ceremonies and endless bonfires and grad parties. It was bittersweet. I finally felt as though I was more accepted and valued by my peers. I was included in more things than usual, and I felt like I was honestly maturing and growing in confidence. I really thought that, maybe, these relationships could continue despite college and the approach of the real world. I dreamed I'd have more opportunities to share my faith with these people. Who knew what was to come? One verse that did bring me comfort was Philippians 1:6: "Being confident of this, that he who began a good work in you will carry it on to completion until the day of Christ Jesus."

CHAPTER 5
Starting Over

(Playlist songs 18 – 26)

I graduated at the perfect time. I took advantage of the self-declared freedom from the past. I shaved off all my hair just to feel like things were different. That summer, I spent so much time going on walks, enjoying the summer rain, and driving around my hometown. I felt happy to be alive. I worked at a pizza shop where the owners always had fun, and I felt like I could be myself. I spent a lot of time with friends just hanging at church, the mall, and playing basketball.

Transitioning out of high school had a profound effect on my faith. It felt like being alive again. I rediscovered my sense of wonder. I hadn't realized until then how much of my late childhood and teenage years had been spent conforming to social fears. It's tough to recall, but I know there were so many forms of entertainment, clubs, and events that I missed out on because I figured I would be humiliated or turned away by them. That may seem ludicrous, but it was a fear that I wished someone had helped me dispel. I wanted to recapture the feeling of being a kid again. I wanted the world to be new. I went back that summer and watched a bunch of old Disney movies and the like. I listened to all kinds of music from the last decade, all for nostalgia's sake. I wanted to rediscover anything important I might've missed.

A last hoorah of sorts for high school was a trip to Orlando, Florida. I went that August with my youth group. My youth group was an important formative experience for me. Every week, a relationship with Jesus was emphasized, and missions were highlighted. We went on a bunch of trips, too. This time, we rented a house in Orlando for the week. It was like an episode of *The Real World* or *Jersey Shore,* packed full of shenanigans. It was a special experience to be on a trip like this with so many of my best friends. We spent a couple days at Disney World, which I highly suggest doing with close friends. So outrageous. The conference was a great experience. We got to hear from amazing speakers, including NFL Hall of Fame coach Tony Dungy. I remember how one speaker explained how one aspect of faith is to understand its role as a relationship. You have to desire intimacy. You have to desire more from God. He won't keep Himself from us. There's a light out there — we won't be left in the dark — it's there for us.

This trip was frustrating, though. Many of my friends got caught up in drama and didn't seem to really care about the conference. They weren't "feeling it." To some, it was just a vacation. Whatever, I guess that's fine; but I ached for the times when we all felt spiritually connected. Those were the moments of true hope for me. The last thing I ever wanted to come off as was self-righteous. I usually felt like the biggest screw up. I was just concerned we weren't being open to hearing from God. I remember one day I was made fun of for a couple different things and out of a large group, only had my friends Jerry, Jenessa, and Megan to hang out with at Disney. (Again — the little things people do for you matter.) *I thought I left high school...*The last night at the conference was a student showcase, and the artist Francesca Battistelli kicked off the show. This was right before she became a major label artist. I heard her song "Free to Be Me," and it stuck with me. I still could go to college and pursue God's call for my own life.

I had a lot of fears going into college. I had chosen to stay relatively local for college. While I was thankful for a lot of privileges high school granted me, I was not alone in worrying we weren't prepared for college academically. I worried about making friends. I'm shy at first (in most cases), and I had been burned by so many toxic relationships before college. I was excited for college to start. I knew I had to put myself into uncomfortable positions to make an impression since I wasn't going to be living with peers.

The college I went to, Waynesburg University, gave us a weekend full of ice-breakers and orientation lectures. I really went out of my comfort zone, talking to most everyone I could. I made some friends (everyone is afraid of not making friends when you start college) who would have me over in the first couple of weeks, and it made a big difference in helping me feel comfortable. I met a girl on day one. Within a week or so, we were dating. My classes started off well. I was pleasantly surprised by how experienced my professors were and their emphasis on the real-world implications for learning. Not that it was always perfect, but this helped set a tone that energized me to learn in college. I had been a lazy student in high school, but I wanted college to be different. My faith was helping me understand there was so much I didn't know and being educated could help me better serve and know God. *He created all of this, so it must matter. I want to understand more.* I tried to take diverse classes throughout college. My major was Psychology, and I liked my music classes so much I minored in it. I took things like government, theatre, guitar (with an amazing guy named Dan with red dreadlocks that hung below his knees), music history, world history, philosophy, and the sciences. A lot of students hate these general education classes, but I wanted to soak in as much as I could. I had largely taken for granted eighteen years of learning opportunities, and it was time to make up for it.

My mind was blown by how much diversity this little college in rural southwestern Pennsylvania opened me up to. The university was nothing like the town I had grown up in, it was its' own world. I met people from Los Angeles, Brooklyn, Dallas, Seattle, and more. Different countries like Bolivia and South Korea, and even a professor from Nigeria were represented. I was thrilled by how many opportunities college was giving me. The college had us take a mandatory freshmen day trip to Washington, D.C., to visit the Holocaust museum. This was an eye-opening experience, which helped me value the human life and the awful tragedies that occur around our world. At the museum, there's this room filled with children's shoes from the concentration camps. It was incredibly heartbreaking to see.

That fall, I took a couple weekend trips with my family to New York City and D.C. again. I was amazed by the sheer complexity of these cities and how rich in culture they were. I had a pipe dream of playing music for a living, and I dreamed of playing in places like this. I wanted to connect with people in these places. *What's it like to actually live here? What are the issues? What does it mean to follow Jesus here? Why does it seem so many people stop believing in God once they get into environments like this?*

My freshmen year was proving to be an interesting year for my relationships. I was so focused on trying to make it in college. I remember my first run through of tests were difficult, but I was learning how to study and be disciplined, and things improved. College was showing me that others were more outgoing and easier to talk to than I had worried about, but I struggled with really connecting. I was basically living out of my car, splitting time between my parent's house, a good drive away, and a separate apartment in my cousin's basement. For some reason, I felt like people knew I was a "commuter," and I had a hard time finding opportunities to get to know people, while others more naturally had roommates, friends at the cafe, etc. I was trying to find my niche at this place. Waynesburg identifies itself as a Christian school, and I experienced culture shock at the diversity in Christian faith I met in peers and faculty at chapel and campus Bible studies. I was unaware at varying perspectives among Christians on what I thought were generally accepted Bible interpretations, social issues, and acceptable behavior. *Wait... some people believe Jesus isn't God? What does He want me to care about? Is God more concerned about saving people or social issues?* College was introducing me to people who called themselves Christians, across the spectrum, from liberal to conservative and everywhere in between. *Okay, what exactly do I believe and why?*

College was having an unpredictable effect on how my faith influenced my relationships. For the sake of privacy, I'll say that one of the relationships/flings I had freshmen year had quickly turned into something I knew it shouldn't, and temptations were mounting. Eventually, I met a breaking point. I had to choose to give in fully to temptations or be true to my convictions. I wish I could say it was an easier choice, but I knew I would have to go at it alone to be myself. One of the hardest things I had to deal with was the drastic change in relationships with my high school friends. What began that year felt like such an unexplainable drift. In a matter of months, some of my closest friends no longer cared about me. A few friends went away for college, and they did not even bother to catch up with me when they returned. These were some of my best friends who didn't bother to even text me. Some of these friends, guys I did everything church-related with, stopped going. Personalities changed.

I knew I was going about things all wrong. I was focusing too much on myself, isolating myself trying to make it at college. Still, from some friends, all I got were midnight drinking invitations from then on out. Maybe declining those opportunities came off as offensive to them, communication was lacking all around. To this day, I don't understand why it seemed like overnight I lost my closest friends. Now, was I a perfect friend? Of course not. I knew there were times I could be selfish and a little awkward, but that's not enough to just drop somebody. To present day, I've experienced a lot of sleepless nights and tears because I built such strong attachment. Old thoughts of *am I expendable?* returned.

Throughout college, I developed a love for John Mayer's music. It helped me keep things in perspective, especially in moments where I'd feel alone. Whenever I'd go home and all I'd have left was my family, the music helped. The song, *Why Georgia,* really described my life. I was trying to figure out if I was living life right — how God wanted me to live. I'd often stop and wonder if I was becoming the man I was meant to be? Do I have the type of character, the sense of integrity, that I want to have? I would have answered no every time. I knew how much I fell short. I was almost constantly being made aware of my immaturities. I was trying to figure out a new environment: I wanted to feel courage, but it was a daily fight against loneliness. My peers seemed close-knit, like they had it all figured out. Was I on the right path? Or was I just screwing it all up?

I soon learned that some high school friends really did care about me, particularly Spenser, Adam, and another friend named Harley. Guys I wasn't especially close with in high school stayed in touch and really tried to connect with me. We quickly became fast friends. Spenser also was going to college at Waynesburg, but he wasn't very involved and had trouble getting to know people. He lived off campus and went home after class. He was a wild guy who spent a lot of time partying. I had made a commitment to still love people, even if I disagreed with their lifestyle. Jesus' love intentionally led Him to hang out with the people who were known as "sinners."

It was impossible not to love Spenser. He's Andy Dwyer from *Parks and Recreation* — I kid you not. I spent all my free time over at his house, playing *Call of Duty,* and laughing for hours. One winter weekend brought on the worst snowstorm I've ever experienced in my life. So much came down, so quickly, that our town was left with no power, no clear roads, and no way to fix either. (And we're used to lots of snow.) Spenser and

I took this opportunity to drive around recklessly in the snow crashing into snow banks. (And no, I never hurt my car, mom.)

I treasured how deeply the guy cared for me. He played football in high school, and I decided I needed his help getting in shape. In high school, I was…not in shape. I couldn't run a mile and usually felt insecure about my appearance. Spenser pushed me past limits. I didn't think I could possibly get through it all. I didn't think it was possible to run a mile. I thought I was too pathetic, too weak. Accomplishing things doesn't come easy, and I found out it's often not simple enough to believe and go for it. Building runner's endurance is painful, and it doesn't get easier — just more bearable. Life seemed a lot like running. Spenser was with me through so much, and thanks to him, I did get into the best shape of my life in my first year of college.

I struggled to find peace with so much uncertainty in my life. I tried going to different events on campus, but I still struggled to find a niche. I remember being so stressed about knowing what I wanted to do with my major after college. I was having an identity crisis. I worried about getting the right classes, having the right grades. My advisor, an awesome Psychology professor named Jenny, always affirmed my craziness, but she always encouraged me to relax. I'm thankful for the people who were patient with me. Some nights, I'd drive back to my apartment, look at the stars, and I'd feel so alive being independent and experiencing new things. Other nights, I'd look up and wonder if I was ever going to find my way, if anyone was going to care about me.

Waynesburg has a Sunday night worship service with live music called Upper Room that is completely student led. Back then, it met in the University's theatre building. I went often and thought this was exactly where I wanted to be. The music was great, and the people seemed cool and passionate about Jesus. I still had a hard time connecting with people, though. Sure, I could make small talk easily, but I still felt invisible — like people didn't really care. I think the Upper Room team's main singer and guitarist, a guy named Dave, must have noticed I came a lot by myself, so he introduced himself. We shared a lot in common, like a love for guitar, and we quickly became great friends. Over the next two years of college, he became one of my best friends and an important mentor. He taught me the joy and frustrations of *FIFA,* and he was great at including me in things, encouraging me to go for risks, and introducing me to people.

One early week during my spring semester, I got invited to hang out with a girl I was getting to know named Rachel. She invited me over to watch the show *Lost* with some friends in one of the girls' halls. having no idea what would happen, I invited Spenser to come; I can be shy after all. We met these girls named Katie and Jaclyn. The five of us really hit it off. Quite possibly the sassiest friendship group ever, but we loved it. We'd do anything to make fun of each other: Spenser can do this thing with puffing out his diaphragm, making it look like he's pregnant, and Katie would freak out every time. Eventually, this evolved into a prank war between Team Anthony/Spenser and Team Girls. We'd mess with each other's cars, rooms, surprise each other with Super Soakers, etc.

We went on a weekend camping trip that Spring, and it was laden with jokes and pranks. What became a staple was this jar of chip-dip. Someone had bought it for a party, and we all thought it was gross. It turned into a prank when I left it hidden by the heater in Rachel's room for a week. This dip ended up in people's cars, purses, and awaiting them in their classrooms. One time, I sewed the dip inside a teddy bear and mailed it to Katie. Our friend Brittany kept it over the first Summer, letting it cook outside on her apartment roof. This nuclear waste previously in the form of dip would continue to be used for pranks for years before it finally was deemed too gross and was retired.

Rachel, Katie, and Jaclyn are still great friends with Spenser and me. They made a huge impact on me my freshmen year by encouraging me in my walk with Christ. Katie's best friend Kylee came to Waynesburg a year later, joined the friend group, prank war, and eventually married Spenser. (You're still welcome, bro!) After everyone went home freshmen year, I remember we all watched the *Lost* finale and did a group chat. I'll never forget that night I sat out on my porch and wept because I was so happy. I don't think I'd ever had more genuine friends in my life.

Freshmen year helped me make more lifelong friends. I made friends with a Pacific islander (don't call him Asian) from Pasadena, CA, named Matt. Matt loves Jesus and music, and we hit it off instantly. I met this bearded wild man with possibly the biggest heart ever named Evan. I was friends with this girl named Brittany, we called her Ginger, who had the craziest story ever. She basically was putting herself through college working numerous side jobs and had just given her life to Jesus in college. She taught me so much about being humble, generous, and thankful. I met a guy named Ben who loved sports and pro wrestling as much as I did. He's one of those genuine friends you always know cares.

I'm convinced these friends helped me get through the first year of college. I knew my mental health was fragile at times. Sometimes, I felt like I was thriving academically and socially. Other times, I would feel overwhelmed. *Do I have what it takes?* I had some intelligent peers who all looked older and seemed to have things figured out. On the other hand, I was sure people thought I looked like a child and knew I had to have been an insecure mess (funny the way our minds work). I started taking advantage of opportunities in our music department and started playing and singing live for the first time. I was petrified. I would feel so nervous, couldn't move my fingers, and my voice trembled terribly. Somehow, I would do okay, and it felt like such a rush. I saved up and bought my dream guitar, a red Gibson Les Paul. For me, I was discovering that music had a purity to it that brought me joy. I didn't care if I wasn't great and was playing simple things. It seemed like such a gift from God, and I believed enjoying it as such and being thankful was honoring to God. My friends helped support me in this, and it meant so much to me. I'll cherish the memories I made just being with these friends, having no responsibility, and doing things like hanging at the college quad or walking around the streets of town that spring.

The Fear of Being Nothing

(Playlist songs 27 – 30)

School ended, and summer came around. I chose to work that summer at a small local grocery store and then the following two summers at a local Walmart. I could have pursued other employment options that could have been more appealing. For example, I could have worked at summer camps. I felt like there was a lot I could learn from being in environments like this, though. Most of my coworkers hadn't pursued higher education, and most of them came from lower income backgrounds. There's a lot of stereotypes of rural communities, especially in our area. We hear a lot about "white trash" and the word "grub." I reckoned it could be a great opportunity to build some relationships with a different kind of people than I was used to, talk about Jesus, and try to help better public businesses in my area if only in small ways. This wasn't popular, and maybe not the best use of my time, but I thought I would grow a lot taking jobs like that.

I never imagined I'd get bored with summer. High school summers were like salvation, but here I was missing people from college. Things were changing in my personal life. I would occasionally see friends, but I'd mainly hang with family and take a couple trips to see college friends. I had too much downtime. I spent a lot of time playing guitar and watching music documentaries. I'd get frustrated because I had these big dreams, but I had the hardest time progressing at guitar or songwriting. It didn't help my insecurities either. On the other hand, my brother Alan had taught himself how to play drums with the game *Rock Band* and was an incredible drummer.

I spent time trying to learn more about concepts in the Bible like redemption, forgiveness, sanctification, justification — a bunch of things I was learning were easy to understand conceptually, but they were intricate and complex with differing Christian perspectives that emerged the more I tried to get a deeper understanding of them. I was trying to reconcile how I should be living after encountering a lot of diversity in college and trying to listen. I was experiencing a dissonance, a feeling of discomfort, because faith was becoming more and more confusing. I mentioned that a lot of friends were becoming increasingly less interested in things related to faith. I'd hangout with people and we'd go to places like Pittsburgh and Morgantown, do things like watch UFC pay-per-views at sports bars. I'd see a lot of people who you could infer weren't Christians, not just doing things like swearing and drinking (why would you expect non-Christians to not do this?), but just in conversations about what mattered in life. *What does Jesus offer that these people need? What matters?* It was confusing for me to wrestle with, and I found it was all too easy for me to shrug it off and assume people were simply rejecting Jesus.

I went back to college and faced a lot of challenges. College became increasingly difficult and busy, but I managed. I spent time doing many of the same things as the previous year like class, playing music, and going to the campus ministries. A lot of my friends were busy, and I started having trouble finding my niche again. I had made friends with a lot of pretty liberal Christians who liked their obscure folk music and their craft beers, which is cool and all if that's you, but it certainly wasn't me. I had never been around people, even those who led ministries, who were so critical of the church. This trend influenced me throughout college and forced me to wrestle with new ideas. I was struggling with church, too. I was usually the only person my age left at my home church. I tried connecting with other groups, like my missionary friends Tim and Katie, but between schedules and family, it just wouldn't stick. I wasn't exactly sure where I fit in belief-wise anymore, so I bounced around between churches, never fully leaving my church back home. At this point, I would have described life as stale. I was around a fair amount of cynicism and indifference at college.

I was losing a sense of wonder when it came to my faith. I was overwhelmed with life. I was doubting if life could be anything more than what I was experiencing. I was doubting if I had to get used to being alone, listening to awful folk music to fit in, and feeling irrelevant in a forgotten town. I was a volunteer tutor for school credit up at an awesome community development organization called The Pittsburgh Project. They work in an impoverished area of Pittsburgh, which was eye opening to experience and meet people. *What hope is there for people here? Are our fates similar? Am I living a comfortable facade?* A lot of people think Pittsburgh is pretty and amazing (fine if you do). I happen to be tougher on the city. I've grown to appreciate a lot about it, but I still think it's a culturally stubborn city. I also think it's a gloomy city. I've heard it described as brooding and foreboding. I was feeling this intensely (in my perception) when I was up there. It wasn't helping my faith.

A few things kept me going. I got on a pretty big U2 and Phil Collins kick, which invigorated me mentally and artistically and helped me on bad days imagine there could still be more than the mundane. Even most days when I'd feel alone, just passing interactions with friends like Dave or Spenser and the girls could turn it around for me. Dave introduced me to a guy we called Sned. The three of us started hanging out a lot. I was struggling with feeling like I made a mistake never leaving my hometown. *Will I ever get out of here?* I clung to believing that God had to have a purpose for me being here.

Taking a Risk

(Playlist songs 31 & 32)

I made it through the winter with my annual bout with depression, or at least minor fight with hopelessness. I wasn't happy living at home. I love my family, but I wasn't independent, and there were too many distractions. My brother and I butted heads a lot. He was in high school, and he wanted me to stop trying to give him life advice. Staying at the apartment wasn't any better. Sure, it had all the amenities in the world, but no one ever wanted to leave campus to hangout. I was going crazy being alone. I still hadn't found an outlet on campus to truly invest in. I tried out for two of the campus ministry worship bands and quite literally was told, "Hey, we think you're swell, but you're not good enough." At least my friend Matt told me don't give up. I started thinking about transferring. Yeah, Waynesburg had its moments, and I would miss friends, but I needed to feel like I wasn't wasting my time.

One day in February, I bumped into one of Spenser's older brothers. He encouraged me to apply for a Resident Assistant position, which is a student job where you get paid to hangout in the dorms and work with campus organizations. A lot of guys I looked up to were RA's, like my friends Evan and Jon (who I mentioned in the first chapter). I thought, *Why not? Everything else I've tried has failed; what's the risk here?* I applied and went through the interview process. I explained I wanted to get to know people so I could serve them and help make their college experience better. I thought that seemed like a practical way of serving like Jesus. Still, I thought there was no way I'd get hired. Here I was, this scrawny kid who nobody interviewing knew. Somehow, apparently, they loved me and hired me. I was going to be assigned the dorm that was historically the athlete party dorm. I asked Spenser if he wanted to move onto campus with me in the fall. He was going through a rough patch personally, wasn't sure if college was his thing, but he surprised me and said yes.

I went into another similar summer with a lot of downtime and a lot of boredom. Another menial job, another annual Dave Matthews concert with my cousin Cindy and our friend Kelly. Then I learned my grandpa had cancer. He was eighty-three, and he always had great health; he was tough as nails. He handled cancer treatment great. Ever since my grandma passed, I tried to be so intentional at spending time with my grandpa and helping him with anything. I tried to value every experience with him.

Between sophomore year and this summer, I had a few flings. One hurt me badly and another was a great friend, but I didn't care to exactly protect against temptations. I learned through this how hypocritical and superficial I could be with my faith. I justified things because I hadn't done "the big one," so God would forgive me. I knew things were off: I had become complacent in my relationship with Jesus. It was easy to know how to act to look spiritual, but I'd feel so empty inside. It was easy to turn morals off and on depending on when it could benefit me. I could have so easily decided to be a people pleaser, go to parties, and have all I was craving. I had to look in the mirror and realize this wasn't the life I knew would be satisfying. I regretted that I had emotionally hurt girls, like I had been hurt before. God wasn't calling me to be that.

I had several fears about going back to school as an RA. I was going to be an authority figure in a hall of football athletes and wrestlers. I felt insecure to be any type of leader. My friend Dave had graduated and committed to a local program by staying a couple years in Waynesburg with other recent grads working in the community and living together in what was called a community house. He really encouraged me to know that God would be with me in this experience.

Almost immediately, being an RA was a great experience. I was getting to train with some incredible peers, many who would become great friends like Sned or another girl named K. I loved being in a place where we were encouraging each other's development and sharing our stories. We had some great supervisors who valued and invested in all of us. My boss (RD) was a guy named Luke. This guy is insane, and he would become one of my best friends. He put some people off by being a conversation dominator, but I learned he was a great guy. Almost every time we would be together, he was encouraging me by sharing stories from scripture and how he has seen God show up in real life. He loved MMA, and we would watch fights together all the time. My time around, Luke taught me that loving people requires sacrifice. Nobody slept less and worked harder than Luke. Was he healthy? Probably not, but Luke focused his energy on others more than anyone I think I've ever met. The first time we ever hung out, we watched the movie *Live Free or Die Hard,* and there's a scene where Bruce Willis is talking about being "the guy." The lesson was leadership isn't about being recognized; it's about doing the right thing for people when no one else but you are there to do it. Luke taught me this every day.

I was assigned a floor of all freshmen guys. Spenser and I both hit it off with everyone. I tried doing little icebreakers to get people to know each other. Eventually, our floor had become tight-knit with a good mix of shenanigans and respect. It wasn't always easy, but I was so thankful to be a part of these friendships. I knew several of the guys were hooked on the show *Lost.* I loved that group of guys. I simply tried to be present with people and ask about their lives. I learned this is incredibly important in any context.

A highlight from junior year was going with Spenser, the girls, and Luke on a school trip to New York City. It was great to be hanging out with friends in Manhattan. The second day there, a Saturday, we went to see *The Lion King* on Broadway. We all dressed up to look nice for the show, had a great time, and afterward, went out for cheesecake. Soon, it was evening, and we decided to walk back up to Times Square. What we didn't realize was at that very moment, while we knew the Occupy Wall Street protests were occurring, this was the only time they had moved to Times Square. We walked right into the middle of it and were curious to see it. What we didn't realize is that we must have looked like lawyer's kids wearing suits and dresses. I had people screaming things at me, getting in my face, and I randomly had these guys at a Muslim booth on the sidewalk calling me slurs. Luke specifically said, "don't get arrested," but I was expecting a fight to break out with this tension, and people were already being arrested around us. We weren't being negative, but I was concerned. I was with a group of mainly females and feared for their safety. We got out of there relatively quickly. It was like being in a movie. All in all, we had a great trip, but this opened my eyes. *Where is God in the midst of chaos, of fear? Is God in control to work this out for good?*

Amazingly, I was experiencing some drastic status changes on campus. I worked with a couple guys on my staff who were incredibly in shape and carried a presence about them. They told me if I treated guys with respect and looked them in the eye, then ninety-nine percent of guys wouldn't give me any trouble. *Apparently, guys are cowards in person?* Sure, there were crazy situations at times like drunk students, but I made friends with types of people I never had before. Before, I never had issues befriending athlete types, but suddenly I was being invited to things I wouldn't have naturally worked my way into, like parties and workouts. This was what Jesus did right? He did life with all kinds of people. Not that I really cared about something as juvenile as popularity, but selfishly, it did feel incredible and affirming. I didn't realize at the time the negative impact it would have on me.

My life changed in the winter. My grandpa had beat cancer like a champ. Unfortunately, chemo had wrecked his immune system. A bout with Pneumonia hit him hard. We had to spend Christmas Day in the hospital together, but he was hanging in there. The prognosis wasn't good, and he started to decline exponentially. Three days later, he passed. I'm incredibly thankful he had such great health that allowed us to do so much together right up until he passed. I'll forever cherish the memories I've made with my grandparents. They taught me unconditional love. I had a hard time during this season. I had lost yet another person from my life. Sometimes life made so much sense, and other times, it would seem completely meaningless. This was one of those seasons where I was wondering where God was.

I was continuing to have a difficult relationship with local churches. I wasn't super invested in one, but I found most to be too political, complacent, and invisible to the community. I knew church was important, and I was meeting sweet people, so I kept going, but I wasn't really learning anything about Jesus or the other big questions about Christianity I was wrestling with. My biggest faith influences were coming from my friends. I had committed to hanging out every Thursday night with Dave and Sned. We were all becoming better friends and agreed we had a cool opportunity to encourage each other's faith journeys. We decided to read different books and studies. We asked each other hard questions about life and could be honest about the good and bad in life. I could get accountability for things like my addiction and ways I was selfish. We continued meeting weekly until Sned and I graduated college.

We did a study looking at the basics of faith—how God desires a loving relationship with us, the importance of trust, living selflessly (this life is not my own), etc. One concept was how God can take our circumstances, even bad, and use them to teach us about His goodness. Not long after reading this, I woke up in the middle of the night feeling like I had been stabbed in the stomach. The pain was awful, but I wanted to try to sleep it off. My boss Luke had told me a story about a guy he knew who had his appendix burst and almost died. Not knowing what was wrong, I called Luke, and he took me to the hospital. Turns out, it was my appendix, and I had surgery.

This would be a relatively low risk surgery, but anything can happen. I had a sense of overwhelming peace throughout the whole process. I believed God was using this experience to teach me to trust Him.

What if my perspective has been small? What if it's just as simple trusting God can use us? Maybe life can be more incredible than I ever actually dreamed it could be? I decided I wanted to move forward with a new understanding: God is the real author of my story, and simply living in confidence of this would make a huge difference. Crazy things started happening in my life. I went from feeling like I was an average student to all of a sudden being informed I was the top student in my major. I won a prestigious award for my major. *What does this mean?* I had people like Luke and supervisors tell me I was a great RA, and I had a great chance at a career in higher-ed (applying for RD jobs) if I chose to pursue that. *You mean I can go to grad school for free?*

I reconnected with a girl named Lauren from high school. We hit it off and connected in a way I never had with anyone before. She was only eighteen and about to leave town for college, so I pulled the "you're too young for me, bro" card, but she encouraged me that what I was learning about faith and sharing with her had made a profound impact. This stuck with me — I wanted to impact people with the love of Jesus. I didn't think it was coincidental the first movie I watched when I had my appendix out was *Back to the Future*. Even though my health wasn't in realistic danger, I felt like I was given a new lease on life. I felt like I was growing and maturing. I wanted to make the most of every opportunity I had left. I joined the school choir, simply because I loved music. This opportunity brought new amazing friends, which opened up a new world of music to discover (Eric Whitacre, for starters). I started trying to support more things on campus. I got really into the campus theatre productions and observed how much effort friends and other peers put into telling stories and embodying characters.

Several shows moved me profoundly, and I was given a whole new perspective on how the arts can impact your life. I tried to go out and support all my athlete friends. I auditioned again and was accepted to join my friend Matt on the Upper Room worship team as a guitarist the next year.

Struggles also came with the new season of success I was experiencing. For instance, I was adamant about having the perfect plan for grad school, even with so much time left in college. I wanted to not have to worry about anything. I wanted control and the feeling of freedom. One time during a study, Dave asked me: Are you serving God because you genuinely want to or because you think He'll give you what you want? I knew what the right answer was, but if I was honest, I was dreaming about bigger and better. *Do I trust that God would have my best interest in mind? Would I miss out? Besides, what could be wrong with gaining success if it's for the Lord?* I didn't realize at the time how self-centered my view was.

I was thankful to take a trip with the college to Jackson, Mississippi, to do community development work and learn from Dr. John M. Perkins. (I would also return a year later.) Dr. Perkins is a renowned civil rights activist, community leader, and pastor. His story growing up dealing with racism and violence is incredibly chronicled in his books. We spent time working on restoring a house for the center. When removing floorboards, I literally fell through a floor weakened by termites. I was fine, and Matt recalls this story as the funniest thing he's ever seen witnessed because of a slow, dramatic yell I let out. Dr. Perkins and other workers told us stories and took us around the city. We learned about civil rights history and visited Medgar Ever's home. What shocked me was to learn how many communities in this part of the country are still segregated. Racism still was alive and well. I was shocked to learn back in the sixties until present day the church either openly supported or were indifferent to racism in these communities. *How can this be?* This was eye opening and convicting to me. *How are Christians to reflect Christ and be active in the community? How do we love our neighbor?*

The Tension

(Playlist songs 33 & 34)

I left junior year feeling like I was ready for the real world. I knew since I had another year, I had more to learn and experience. I wanted to make the most of it. Part of me was really looking forward to moving on from southwestern Pennsylvania, and I wanted to go out in style. I had decided I wanted to go to graduate school at a particular big, conservative Christian school. In wrestling with many of my faith questions, I decided it was best to be bold for Jesus. I should be unashamed of Him, and I should make no apologies about serving Him. What was wrong with the world is that they didn't know Jesus. I decided since I was doing well in Psychology, I would be a Christian counselor so I could help people and hopefully point to Jesus and actually be paid for it. This sounded like a comfortable plan, where I could talk about Jesus, but keep my hands clean while the world around me burned. I was reading into a lot of things about culture and different end times interpretations of scripture. I even watched those Kirk Cameron *Left Behind* movies. I concluded clearly people need Jesus, and this was my plan. Life was about to teach me, however, while maybe I understood some big picture concepts, my perspective was narrow, my compassion was lacking, and I hadn't realized how much of a cultural bubble I was living in.

My summer went slow until I took a trip out west in early August to see my uncle Bill and Aunt Char. We took a road trip to see Yellowstone, stopping at Idaho Falls, the Grand Tetons, and Jackson Hole along the way. It is an unbelievable country. We got to see all kinds of wildlife including bear, moose, bison, and more. I got to climb up a rock hill called Sheepeaters Cliff. I remember I backed from view of my uncle at the top and cried because I wished my grandparents could have been there to see who I was becoming. I never dreamed life could be this good. Once back at their home in Utah, we enjoyed the sun and spent plenty of time biking and golfing. A real highlight was going early one morning to hike up Mount Timpanogos. At my uncle's encouragement, I decided I wanted to be a little crazy and swim in Emerald Lake, which is a lake of water melt near the summit from a rock glacier in the mountain. I hopped in and swam out about five yards before trying to swim back. It was so cold my body locked up, and I had a few doubts I could swim back. Within a minute or two, the August sun had dried me, and I felt amazing. *What good is life if you don't do a few crazy things?*

My uncle Bill imprinted a lot of important lessons onto me, such as personal responsibility and accountability, questioning everything, and the best stuff in life being experiences not things. I remember being up there and looking down on the valley realizing this was a literal and figurative mountaintop experience. As tempting as it was to try to cater my life to comforts and personal goals, like staying in a place where I can hike mountains all the time, I understood it's not meant to last. I was called to go back to where the need is. I believed Jesus calls us to be with people and to see the needs right where you are.

I went back to college motivated to give back and to understand the purpose of coming back for one last year. I remember spending time with Harley, Adam, and Spenser before school started and felt like everything was coming together as I was entering adulthood. It was an exciting time. I looked forward to leveraging relationships at school and sharing about Jesus more. I returned as an RA and would be serving my last year in a relatively new apartment/suite style building (compared to the sixty-five-year-old building I had previously served in). Luke was my boss again, and I worked with an amazing staff — my friends Sned, Blair, Derrick, and Warner.

We were a dream team. This staff became incredibly close and often studied together or stayed up all night talking about things like *The Walking Dead*, politics, and Jesus.

I tried to give back to as much as I could. I had begun playing and serving with the Upper Room worship band. Matt and I took advantage of opportunities to play music as often as possible. I helped with Bible studies and prayer groups. These avenues were allowing the opportunity to develop closer relationships with younger students so I could share what God had been doing in my life. I had an internship with my professor, Keith's, private counseling practice. I also had a year-long history of music class, which basically could have been called the history of everything. I still involved myself in choir and other interactive music department events like educational symposiums. These were learning opportunities where I was the connection of how being better educated and cultured made me better able to serve and relate to people. I did struggle with balancing everything. Spenser and the girls were mad at me for not spending time with them. I was simply spread too thin.

I was happy to be building good relationships with many different friend groups. I had several almost-relationships with girls, but either through my own hesitation or chemistry issues, they didn't work out. These things were all handled maturely, and healthy friendships were maintained. My confidence grew, and more friendship doors were opened. Still, I couldn't help but wonder when I was going to find someone. *When will somebody love me just for being me?* I did have great friends like Dave, Matt and Sned, but sometimes I'd feel alone. *I'm being impatient and paranoid.*

I spent a lot of time trying to hang out with athletes that lived in my building, a population notorious for not attending educational or religious events at Waynesburg. I learned trust in relationships is everything. I felt like I was called to do something out of my comfort zone and to be with people I wasn't naturally going to be with. I connected with a new RD working at the school, a guy named Chris, who told me about how he was going to coach a new club lacrosse team at the school, and a core group of students had already committed. Growing up, that sport always intrigued me, but it wasn't offered locally. I jumped in learning the skills and rules. I had a lot of fears. I didn't think I could compete physically or keep up cardio-wise. I worried about serious injury, considering I was playing with guys who played other sports like football and wrestling. *Also, who wants to get smacked constantly with a metal stick?* I certainly had my challenges physically, but I found a niche skill wise. I set a goal to be like a basketball point guard — to make the team better and assist the scorers. We played our first season that spring and had a difficult time. Our first game was against a school who competed for national championships at the club level. (Many major colleges and universities lack varsity lacrosse teams.) We were crushed 28-0. We continued growing (through a lot of fighting and sloppy all-around effort). We did win one game and finished the season playing better. I only ever scored goals in practices but took pride in accumulating assists and drawing penalties. It was a joy just to be able to play.

The team we built was a real motley crew. A large percentage of my teammates felt like scoring girls and partying is what life was about. The most heinous of "locker room talk" was normal. Still, I loved these guys. Each one brought something incredible, and I was learning to see more the potential in people. I'd often lead team prayers and would be jokingly referred to as "Reverend." Sometimes, I'd feel disrespected. I wasn't a physical player, so I'd be treated as if I was soft. I tried befriending and caring for some of the socially awkward players on the team. This made me the brunt of jokes. A lot of teammates respected my faith, but I think they viewed me less seriously. I never was an in your face guy about it and would try to naturally work low-pressure faith questions into one-on-one conversations. Still, sometimes I felt like my teammates viewed matters of faith as irrelevant, and by association, this made me somewhat of a joke in their eyes. "Alright, Reverend," some would smirk at unrelated comments. This, coupled with very underdeveloped lacrosse skills, gave (mostly younger) teammates the green light to disrespect me. It was challenging to not throw insults back or say similarly harsh things. My one purpose for playing was to point my teammates to Jesus. I'm sure swearing at them would have caught them off guard and set it straight, but what good would that have done? I credit coach Chris and my teammate Joe for making it through the outside winter practices and tough teammates relationships. Joe always smiled, joked, and in general took a Happy Gilmore approach to everything. They kept me sane.

Lacrosse wasn't the only place I had trouble feeling successful in being a Christian example. The more people I met, the more diversity and barriers to faith I found. *Why is it so many people can seem totally indifferent to matters of faith?* I struggled with working so hard on events only to have no impact, regardless of how we spun evaluation processes. I thought about my own struggles with church and wondered if it helped me grow closer to Jesus. I remember wondering if I wasn't Christian, then how would I be attracted to church. I couldn't answer that. *What does Jesus offer that ought to impact everyone? Is grace, when understood, truly irresistible? Is the church failing?* Some days, I would feel so connected to God. Other days, I'd wonder if anything we were doing in our churches or at school mattered to anyone outside. I felt a tension. We read about and see these big churches talking about how God can move and do incredible things. *Why can't it happen here? CAN it happen here; is there even a God? Hey now, Anthony, stop that thinking.* The 2012 national election came and went, and I struggled with many Christian voices I had been influenced by. *Are we ultimately about Jesus and what scripture says, or are we more concerned with political bias (without looking truly at Jesus)? Have I been listening to wrong or immature teaching?* A lot of pressure was mounting. *Am I screwing things up? Am I not spiritual enough to properly minister to my friends. Am I wasting time?* Part of me was ready to bounce out of town and cut ties, and yet my heart was breaking for the people around me. *We can be so much more, but we choose to think we have it all together; we choose to think we aren't sinners. Jesus forgive us all.*

For the sake of privacy, I will say the following occurred sometime during my senior year. It was a Friday night with nothing to do. A girl I had just met texted me, asking if we could hang out. It was her birthday. I didn't think anything of it, so I said sure. We meet up and talked a little. I asked her what she wanted to do. She smiled and started kissing me. *Okay, I'm down with this.* Eventually, we paused. I laughed and asked her what she wanted (thinking this is a little too good). "Birthday sex," she answers. *Ahhh what?* I have no idea what happened. Did I stop to think about the importance of why I had waited the first twenty-one years of my life? Did I think about how it might affect my relationship with Jesus? Maybe it was years of porn addiction that made it easy for my brain to shut off. Maybe I just wanted it. Long story short, I lost the big one that night.

It's hard to describe how I felt the next day — scared mostly. Some of you reading may think this is rather tame. After all, not many wait. It's not the end of the world and certainly not unforgivable. Many see no issue here. For me, it represented something bigger. Yes, I had wanted to wait for marriage for important benefits like purity and relational trust. On another level, though, this seemed like I had committed an act of treason against Jesus. It was like my actions said, "Jesus I don't care what you had to endure or what you want for me, my desires are more important." As crazy as it may sound, I felt like I had committed a major crime. If the police showed up and took me away, I would have accepted it. This was the guilt I felt. Maybe for the first time, I realized how ugly sin is to God. I made a choice that communicated, "God, you aren't good enough."

This severely affected me through my senior year. *I'm a hypocrite. What if people knew?* I believed I disappointed God, and He was angry with me. I kept on trying to serve, care for relationships, and move forward with what I thought I was supposed to do, but things didn't seem so clear anymore. I had suffocating guilt. I wanted to cling to hope, to have the Holy Spirit heal me. I was approaching graduation, and I started second-guessing everything. I applied to higher-ed jobs and graduate assistantship positions, things I thought I had amazing references and connections for, but nothing worked out. Through experiences in my internship and in reading, I started second-guessing the career path I had choose. *What if counseling is not what I think it is?* I thought I was going into a field with a lot of freedom of expression and practice, but I was finding the extreme opposite. I still was accepted into several graduate programs, but I couldn't decide on a choice. *Where is my best fit? How can I live somewhere else when I never have moved?*

I even had strange coincidences happening, like professors telling me it would be a mistake to do certain things or even an admissions woman from one school calling me while I was visiting a different school I was favoring to tell me I was crazy if I attended such a program. *What is going on here?* I started realizing just how much debt I would be in coupled with projected earnings in counseling. *How am I ever going to afford to pay off anything or provide for a family?* I had lived under the idea everything would work out fine. *What if I've been irresponsible?* I remember being afraid of moving away from my family. *Am I still just a scared little kid?*

My last days of college were spent celebrating and investing in all the different friend groups I had made at college. I valued time with RA's, Upper Room, lacrosse, choir, Bible studies, etc. I really had a hard time saying goodbye to a lot of peers and mentors, particularly the ones staying behind. I remember seeing a lot of peers ready to graduate and feeling sad. *These people went to a Christian college, and it seems like Jesus made no impact on them. Did I fail in being a witness? Did I waste my time?* One of the last days at college, I played in another music concert, and I sang a stripped down acoustic cover of the U2 song, "I Still Haven't Found What I'm Looking For." (Okay, maybe I was being overly dramatic — hindsight people.) I made my friend Liz cry. Apparently, it was good, and afterward, one my favorite professors we called Dr. D., who was like a mom figure to us, came up to me and just encouraged me by saying, "You'll find it, baby." As meaningful as that was, I wish I would have trusted it. The night before graduation, I had my first panic attack.

CHAPTER 6
What Now

(Playlist songs 35 – 39)

I entered post college life with a sense of optimism. *Any day now I'll make a grad school choice where everything will just make sense again.* It was nice to have options, but I was constantly feeling anxious and out of time. I sought counsel from different mentors; I even looked online for scriptural encouragement. Most avenues kept coming back to, "Trust the Lord, and He will make your path straight" (and other similar paraphrases of Prov. 3:6). Here was the issue: I thought I was trusting the Lord, but my path was downright invisible. The thought that kept haunting me was this: *God is disappointed and angry at me. I failed Him.*

I remember meeting up with my friend Lauren. Whatever I decided for graduate school, I knew I was going to move away, so she wanted to see me before life happened. We went to get frozen yogurt, and I heard all about her freshmen year at college. I had never met someone so thoughtful and genuinely interested in what God was teaching me. I left that night wondering if she was the perfect girl for me, but I knew life circumstances would never work out. *What is God doing with me?*

At least one thing had to go like expected. For my graduation, my Aunt Frances generously offered to take my mom and I to Italy. We signed up to go with a guided group from Venice down to Florence and eventually finish in Rome. I met some incredible people in our group in Italy, particularly Jeff and Denise who are executives for a well-known high-end hotel chain, an elderly couple named Sheri and Don, and a pair of sisters around my age — Emma and Olivia. Throughout the trip, we saw magnificent historical buildings, churches, artwork, and ate incredible food. Venice provided amazing opportunities to take gondola rides, eat tons of gelato, and even see glass blowers practice their craft on the island of Morano. From there, we went to Padua, stopped to see the Villa Pisano estate and the Scrovegni chapel. We took a high-speed train down to Florence next. This was an incredibly walkable city with a lot of history, like Michelangelo's *David* sculpture and Da Vinci 's art. Florence highlights included climbing up the Duomo with the sisters and overlooking the whole city, visiting a Tuscan vineyard owned by the Frescobaldi family, and having a private concert at the home of Italian pianist Gregorio Nardi. At this point, I knew we were being quite spoiled. We ended our trip in Rome. It was breathtaking to see the Pantheon, Vatican, Sistine Chapel, Trevi Fountain, Spanish Steps, and Coliseum. We also learned how to make Italian gnocchi in a cooking class.

Overall, I had an amazing time in Italy, but I struggled with not seeing much in terms of faith expression in the country. This was supposed to be a predominantly Christian nation compared to other surrounding nations of different, or no faith, and it seemed like all I ever saw in terms of churches were now museums. *Is God really present everywhere? How is He moving around the world?* I knew I had to go back home and face reality. I couldn't stay in Italy and watch international soccer forever. I had questions to answer and life to get on with. However, things were growing more and more uncertain.

Unsure of what to do upon arriving back home, I kept working my summer job at Walmart. I lived most days with a sense of never-ending anxiety. *I have to figure something out.* Everything seemed like a bad idea or too risky when thinking about job outcomes, money, etc. Eventually, my job performance began to dive. I didn't care about what I was doing. My mind was elsewhere. I spent a lot of days going to work and then coming home and lying on the couch for hours, feeling paralyzed by fear. I realized that all my joy had been robbed, but I couldn't figure out how to get it back. *What does God want from me? What can I do for Him?* I was wrestling with the spiritual questions Italy presented, and I couldn't reconcile them. I'd catch a couple things on those Christian TV channels about missions internationally and engaging culture domestically, and honestly, it seemed fake. It seemed too good to be true. *So, it's just about saying a prayer with a few words? Is that really God changing lives?*

I began to doubt. I listened to music I had loved for a long time and current worship music, and I felt doubt. These were songs about this all powerful, always present God in control, and I wondered if maybe it was too good to be true. *Is this reality?* Popular Christian bands and churches I paid attention to suddenly seemed over the top, contrived, and my sense of gravitas had faded. As the summer wore on, I started feeling immense self-doubt and wondering where God was. I had tentatively planned on moving to a school in Virginia Beach, but I got to a breaking point with anxiety where I decided I couldn't do it. I wanted to stay home, try to work in the mental health field, and figure things out. My family thought I was crazy and living scared. And, admittedly, I was.

I was becoming more confused and frustrated with the church by the day. *Why are there so many different churches and competing theological voices? Is any of this real? Who do you believe?* I had struggled for a while with thinking about how local churches, especially ones I had seen in rural areas like mine, were increasingly out of touch with their communities. I don't mean doctrinally; I mean a non-Christian likely wouldn't be able to articulate any reason at all why they would consider going to church. I maintained great relationships with my pastors back at my home church, but I struggled with feeling like the work they did was invisible, and this only fueled my doubts. I watched the movie adaptation of *Blue Like Jazz* and left what was meant to be an eye-opening movie of optimism wondering if I was following one big joke? I had no community back home. My church had few attendants my age, and those who were seemed like they had zero interest in being friends. *Is all of this a joke? Has any of this ever been real?*

I wondered if I had been duped into following some type of American political movement disguised as an ancient Middle-Eastern religion. I even visited other churches and felt completely invisible. *Does anyone care that I'm here? I thought church was about caring for the hurting: Well, here I am!* The social ladder is supposed to be nonexistent in God's Kingdom, but I kept seeing it. Of course, there could never be a perfect church, but I knew social ladder selfishness had permeated my youth experience. Now I was more aware than ever how it affected church. "Anthony, what are you doing now?" I couldn't help but believe people didn't really care I was struggling. Was I meeting people's expectations of being a failure? I was dying for somebody to give me hope.

I'll never forget the feeling of August rolling back around and seeing college students coming back while I was still working at Walmart. (I mean no disrespect to employees in industries like this, you are some of the greatest people — and we are all more than job titles.) I had become so disoriented and emotionally paralyzed by how far off course my life had drifted. I was embarrassed and felt like a failure. I still couldn't come up with any goals or dreams that seemed to make sense. People asked me if I considered ministry, but I didn't feel called. I really didn't feel "anointed," "special," or "worthy." I was a screw-up and not a poster child. I had my own doubts about faith anyways. I went through a phase of binge watching the show *Breaking Bad* with my brother. The show is gripping, well-written, and very dark. I think it influenced me a little too much. *Maybe life really is a bunch of pain and disappointment. Maybe it's just a bunch a selfish people hurting others to survive. Maybe none of this has any meaning.*

Suddenly, I felt very alone in the world. It had been almost ten years since I had felt such an existential crisis. I remember walking along the forest and feeling scared. *What if I am just alone here in this cold, dark wasteland?* I suddenly felt very weak and vulnerable. I remember one time Dave came over to visit and wanted to do one of our typical Bible studies, this time on purity. *Dave, what is the point? None of this matters! This is just more meaningless nonsense about manhood and other irrelevant church agendas.* I was entering a dark place mentally. The video game *Grand Theft Auto Five* came out, and I played it with Harley a bunch. Harley had just moved to take a great job, marry a great girl named Megan, and live on the beach in Florida. (If life is a race to the top, he wins.) I wondered if I would ever have the chance to be happy again. Was I stuck living a life of pain? *I must have screwed up God's plan for me, and now I'm being punished.* The video game featured the Phil Collins' song "I Don't Care Anymore." I thought it was oddly fitting.

Eventually, I did land a job at a mental health hospital doing in-patient counseling. I felt like I was living in a different world. I got to interact with doctors, nurses, psychologists, and even business managers. Weirdly, it was a disappointment. Everything seemed so focused on money and strict treatment requirements. (Oddly, I was told day one I couldn't talk about faith just because an assumption was made from the college on my resume. Coincidence?) I felt like patients were treated like animals, not people. I was criticized for wanting to be everybody's friend. *How do people get help if they are not cared for and treated like human beings?* Soon, I started to feel like I was the patient — like I was a prisoner. I had become disillusioned with life. Is there any hope for our communities or our people? Is the dream to grow up and suffer every day to make barely livable salaries? I would walk around the hospital campus (combined with others in a complex) talking with coworkers and seeing thousands of university students daily. I couldn't help but wonder if the majority didn't view partying, sex, and money as the highest goals of living. Even a disillusioned guy like me couldn't get excited about that. *Where does Jesus even begin to fit in?*

I worried about my brother Alan who had left college and was bouncing between oilfield jobs. *How does anyone make it anymore?* Even small comforts were turning out to be hollow. Alan and I would always take friends to this amazing Chinese buffet to get this over the top good Coconut Shrimp (creamy style), which we had renamed Shrump after an over the top billionaire — listen, our humor is weird, and we couldn't predict the future. Even Shrump couldn't make me happy. (I tried this route a lot and gained a lot of weight.) On a serious note, I'd pay attention to surrounding aesthetic of fast food, decaying infrastructure, and bizarre advertisements and wonder: *What hope is there for real meaning in life? Were we all doomed to the boredom of monotonous suburban life?*

My life had spiraled out of control. I was ashamed of what I had become. I was living completely out of fear. Even just nine months out of college, I felt like a shell of the person I was in college. *Was any of that even real? Did college happen?* I felt like a completely different person, someone who was successful in a bubble, but now I was lost. A couple of times I tried going back to visit and something just felt very wrong inside me. I didn't try to be involved in the social scene or anything drastic, but even physically being on campus made me feel insecure and unwelcome. An exile. What would bring me back for short periods of time was catching up with friends. Strangely, I would feel like myself anytime I was with them. Friends like Chris the RD and lacrosse coach, Matt, my old coworkers Derrick and Warner, a nurse named Lynae, and siblings CJ and Caiti, Kayla and Rusty. I also really connected with a professor's family at Waynesburg. Mick was a business professor there, his wife Andrea was attending ministry school with their daughter Emily, and the other daughter Audrey went to WU. This family was incredibly hospitable to students and were the first example I had seen in a long time of genuine, caring Spirit-led people. They loved people and Jesus. They gave me hope maybe all was not lost. These people helped remind me there still were people out there who cared I existed. These opportunities were few and precious, and this peace would only last so long.

Many days, I would weep on the way to work. I felt out of control. I had panic attacks where I couldn't breathe. During these attacks, I'd have intense feelings of abandonment, feeling forgotten, like I was trapped in suffering. *You did this to yourself, Anthony. You deserve all of this.* My cousin Gary offered me a job, and I was so paralyzed by fear and unable to imagine me doing anything, I had another panic attack just because of the idea. I honestly thought I was losing my mind. Cindy had taken in a kitten who lost its mother, and I remember being alone with it and weeping. It was scared and wanted its mother. I felt just as vulnerable. *What is happening to me?*

I had to spend many nights at work in sixteen-hour shifts to help watch patients. I'd sit there in the dark, wondering if I had any hope. Several nights I'd do this and watch huge snowfalls outside the window. *This is either one of God's wonders, or this is nothing. Am I alone?* I couldn't help wondering if I had wasted all the opportunities I ever had. I thought of my grandparents and parents. All the sacrifices they made, years of endless work and tears. *Have I wasted all of it?* I remember driving to work one day and seeing thousands of people walking along the street in the other direction back to attend a college basketball game. *This must be like what the church is in culture. If I'm a Christian, then these people on the other side probably aren't. I wonder if the divide is that large. How could the church, or even God, ever overcome such an impossible scenario?* I decided that I needed to figure out what I believed. Does this faith stuff make sense or not? If not, then life probably isn't worth living.

CHAPTER 7
Found

(Playlist songs 40 & 41)

Right before I took the mental health job, I had a question I knew my friend Lauren could answer. Honestly, I was embarrassed to call her. Here was this amazing girl off at college in Nashville, so why would she care to talk to me? *I'm the loser she left behind.* I was intrigued but doubtful she would still care about me. *There's no way she would still be interested in my life.* To my surprise, we began talking a lot. She came home for Thanksgiving, and we hung out. I was even more surprised when she explained she still had feelings for me. *You've got to be kidding me.* I couldn't understand why. She would say the sweetest things like I loved people and Jesus so well. *You really don't know me.* She made her intentions clear about wanting to date me. I thought she was crazy. Here I was feeling like a total failure. I (should have been thankful) was embarrassed to still be working at Walmart after graduating college. I believed my peers viewed me as a failure, as worthless. Why didn't Lauren think the same? *She's just blinded by a crush; she doesn't realize she can do so much better.* I assumed in a place like Nashville she would meet intelligent, successful, and attractive guys. She explained that she had, but no one ever measured up to me. I couldn't believe it. I made so many excuses why I couldn't date her. She was a college sophomore living ten hours away. I was still trying to find a way to move away and get on with life. I felt so awkward because she was younger, and I worried people from high school would be judgmental about a potential relationship. She was stubborn though and persisted in saying my reasons weren't valid. She said there was no risk in taking a chance. I told her I couldn't do it.

Work gave me a lot of downtime, especially the multiple times per week I worked sixteen-hour overnight shifts. I had never had this kind of time, so I decided I wanted to read a few books. In college, I read a couple book on my own, but I was never a big reader. I decided I needed to figure out faith, so an obvious step was to read books written by pastors about faith. I started by rereading some old Donald Miller books and remembered why I loved them in college. *This really is intriguing. I want to believe this; I want to have a faith that makes sense.* I started reading a bunch of books about Christian living. I don't even remember exactly which book or moment, but I came to a place where I was moved profoundly by what I was reading. All I remember is it being a simple explanation of Christianity and practical ways a church was living it out. *This is what I want. I want a genuine faith that makes sense in the real world. I want to anchor my life to this.*

I started rediscovering the basic beliefs of Christianity. Jesus as God's son died for our sins. Jesus rose again and gives us hope that He has authority over everything. If we profess honest faith in Him and follow Him with our lives, we will be with Him forever. We are saved from the punishment we deserve. God loves us so much that He paid the price for the punishment we deserve. I read books on what is called apologetics, or understanding if you can trust that the claims of Christianity are true. My mind was blown over the historical evidence supporting Biblical accounts of Gospel witnesses, combined with the hundreds of Old Testament prophecies only Jesus could have fulfilled.

I read books about Jesus' character. I came back to a popular passage I had known. In Matthew chapter 11, Jesus says, "Come to me, all you who are weary and burdened, and I will give you rest. Take my yoke upon you, and learn from me, for I am gentle and humble in heart, and you will find rest for your souls. For my yoke is easy, and my burden is light." I knew I could trust this. I knew through all the noise, all the ways people had clouded my idea of God, this was Jesus, and He is real. Jesus wants me to let Him be everything.

Another passage that helped me put my life and relationship with God in perspective is 1 Timothy 1:15-17. It says, "Here is a trustworthy saying that deserves full acceptance: Christ Jesus came into the world to save sinners — of whom I am the worst. But for that very reason I was shown mercy so that in me, the worst of sinners, Christ Jesus might display his immense patience as an example for those who would believe in him and receive eternal life. Now to the King eternal, immortal, invisible, the only God, be honor and glory for ever and ever. Amen." I found personal healing through this. I read the popular passage Psalm 23. I was blown away. *Is this truth for someone as insignificant as me?* These became life verses for me. I didn't have to be defined by my mistakes or pain but through identifying with Jesus. I had really developed an insatiable desire for reading. I was learning much about the story of God. I was discovering He is the greatest source of joy I could ever experience, and I could live passionately in everything I do for His glory. I would read books about the work missionaries are doing around the world and the impossible ways and circumstances God was showing up and proving faithful to the people He called. My heart was breaking with optimism.

Slowly it seemed like things began coming back online. It wasn't overnight, but I realized I had recommitted my life. I knew Jesus is real. Jesus was giving me peace and comfort, like the presence of a relationship I thought I had lost. I was being reminded of the wonderful people that were still in my life. I was learning, even if I caused it, God could take my mistakes and pain and redeem all of it.

I was learning to live in a new sense of confidence and optimism, but it wasn't easy. It required a lot of prayer. I'd walk around in public and fight a feeling that questioned, "Is life all too random and chaotic for God to really be in control?" I felt a sense of emptiness like what T.S. Eliot described in his poem, "The Hollow Man." I still had a lot of questions. What is the purpose and hope for people like the patients I worked with at the hospital? How is God building the church in America? What I knew was that God was breathing new life into me. I seriously could breathe again without feeling a weight on me. So much was being reaffirmed from my life of what I had experienced and learned. My experiences have been real, and God has provided. *My life and faith are not accidents.* I wondered what I was supposed to do about it. I knew back in high school I ran from ministry. I wanted to live a comfortable life, and I was made to feel like I was less special than others. I had my doubts about my own ability or my worthiness to go into vocational ministry. I had moments where I prayed the biggest, boldest prayers. I wanted to see God move so mightily and see whole cities be alive with the hope of Jesus. I wanted to play any part I could. I wanted to "chase lions." I remember one night sitting out looking at the stars, listening to some of my favorite ambient film soundtracks, and just feeling like my heart was going to explode dreaming and praying. I still had fears and old insecurities that reared their ugly heads. My friends Mick and Andrea helped me work out God's rich love as our Heavenly Father. They helped me realize God could do anything, and the only barriers to living a life of ministry were created in my head. Lauren helped convince me I had a small view of God, that I was underestimating Him. Whatever He was calling me to do, He would be faithful. I had a future to look forward to. I could be myself and let God craft his own unique life for me.

My friendship had grown with Lauren. She knew more things about me than anyone else. She had seen the ugliness in my life and still chose to pursue me. She encouraged me to pursue Jesus and valued this aspect of life more than I had ever experienced in a dating sense. Somehow, I soon realized how incredible she is, and despite all my excuses and fears, decided to date her. I include her in this book because of her priceless impact on my life, previously mentioned and detailed in the following chapters. At time of writing this, we are still dating, crazy in love, and the stated (hopefully near) goal is marriage. It could be strange to write about a girl who isn't yet your wife, but regardless of how life may play out, Lauren has changed my life, and for that reason alone, is worth recording. I thank God daily for her and that He used her to save my life and my faith. I've continued growing and living (which I'll get to), and we have had amazing experiences as a couple. I have also been very human, full of fears and real shortcomings, and have hurt her as a result. Still, she has taught me so much about unconditional love, forgiveness, and patience. She has cared for me in ways I never experienced before. *Everyone leaves me.* Lauren has cared for my healing, restoration, and growth. She has loved me for me. I have never known someone who has taught me the love of Jesus through their life more than her. I cannot predict the future, but I can reflect and say, "Thank you for everything. Thank you for loving me so well."

CHAPTER 8
All In

(Playlist songs 42 – 44)

If this is real, and I'm committed, then my life must be different. If I really was trusting Jesus with my life, then my actions needed to reflect I believed it. I had read plenty of Mark Batterson books to understand that. I really believed God was calling me into vocational ministry. While I believe anything can be ministry, this was a sense I couldn't shake. I never imagined being a pastor was something I would pursue, but here I was feeling like I'd never be fulfilled if I didn't do it. I quit my job at the hospital with nothing lined up. I figured I would work for a friend at this amazing summer camp ministry in an impoverished, forgotten area of Waynesburg, and then I decided I'd be off for seminary. I had to make literal steps of faith. I couldn't imagine any way things could work out, but I wanted to trust God. I still had doubts and fears. I had days which would be best described as anxious. *Opportunity seems scarce, packaged, and controlled. How does anyone break through the mold? How do you make a difference?*

What began to happen was amazing. I began to make an intentional effort, which developed in focus over the next year, and continues to present day. This effort was to understand my identity in Jesus. I continued to study and focus on the core beliefs (truths) of Christianity. *What has Jesus done for me? Who is He?* I wanted to be known by the declarations I found in Romans chapters five and six. I wanted to live in joy and identity like the man in Matthew 13: 44, "The kingdom of heaven is like treasure hidden in a field. When a man found it, he hid it again, and then in his joy went and sold all he had and bought that field." It was like I was meeting Jesus for the first time. It was like I was experiencing a new life. I began to grow in confidence (a sense of peace, not arrogance) as I focused on this in the next year, and I still cling to this.

One morning in June, at 9 a.m., I was working at camp when I received a call from an RD, my friend Ashley, at Waynesburg where I did my undergrad. She explained an RD position had unexpectedly become open, and I was the first person she was told to contact. *What is the meaning of this?* Somehow, I knew the job was mine if I wanted it. *No way I want to go back, I want to get out of here! What about being called to ministry? Would I be welcomed and remembered if I went back?* Everything about the interview process seemed unbelievable. I didn't feel qualified and felt like I was shooting from the hip on everything. Apparently, they loved it. *Life is a comedy.* It's like a movie where somehow the idiot gets the job. I was honest about my convictions, and how I believe community is everything. I remembered how my old boss Luke had made such an impact on me and how he lived ministry. *There must be a reason God wants me to do this.* So, I went back.

The job of a Resident Director is an insane mix of responsibilities. It is like being a 24/7 landlord, mentor, counselor, medical first responder, educator, event planner, investigator, constant communicator, and office administrator. I had plenty of fears about my ability to do the job and how I would be received. I was blown away by the almost immediate response. I was working for my friends Chris and Kelley — married employees who first believed and invested in me when I was a college freshman. I was thrilled to now be coworkers with old friends Chris (my Lacrosse coach), Russ, and Ashley. My friend Matt also was hired to work at the school the same time I was. Matt had a similarly difficult year, and it felt like such a gift to see God taking care of both of us. Amazingly, I was treated with such dignity and respect by my fellow employees. It was a long time since I had felt such a feeling.

It's difficult to describe the impact being back in an environment of dreamers did for me. Being an RD opened new worlds of opportunity. Over several years now, I have had the opportunity to work with thousands of students. These relationships, like the RA's I've had the privilege of working with, have brought so much joy to my life. I cannot even begin to name all the students who have impacted my life (basically all of you), and I hope I have returned the favor. Students who knew me as a student gave me professional respect and helped me feel like I wasn't forgotten. Time was needed to become comfortable in the role. I was given the opportunity to oversee several campus ministries and work with amazing teams of students. I felt capable but unqualified to lead these. I primarily focused on pointing people to Jesus and helping students understand they are somebody; their lives matter. I've used some great resources over the years, and I feel like the Holy Spirit has given me the words to say in conversations that matter, but this simple approach is all I've done. I'm not an expert, and I haven't pretended to be. I want to see people study and experience Jesus for themselves. He changes lives. I also was given an unbelievable opportunity to go back and coach lacrosse with my coworker Chris. I had progressed in my knowledge of the game and again was blown away by how relationships reconnected and developed with my former teammates. We eventually built a successful playoff team. I think focusing on building up others and helping them understand their worth is so important in their development. There is just something about caring for someone else's life. Not many people have others that truly care and are invested in their life. I've found it makes a huge difference.

Responsibilities were forcing me to do some growing up. I had to act with integrity and accountability now more than ever, but I fell short in many ways. Different experiences and choices brought me face to face with my sin, with my ugliness. *Am I going to be the person I'm meant to be?* I had to go through a season of repentance, of confession, of healing. I've never been a perfect person, but I was learning Jesus never leaves us even during our worst choices. God's correction is not for our demise, but for our rehabilitation. God wants me to be reconciled to Him, so I can walk with Him and let Him fulfill His purposes through me. This changed a lot for me when I learned this. I could let go of who I've been and not live in fear of screwing up.

I've been pushed further than I ever imagined possible in my job. God has taught me so much having to lead trips and events, for example. I'm thankful for plans failing so I could learn to remain calm and poised. Visiting Nashville to see Lauren particularly helped me realize the work God was doing in my life. God was breathing a new confidence for me in Him, and it was stripping my insecurities away like never before. I remember sitting in a Nashville coffee shop, looking around and seeing beautiful and seemingly successful young adults and feeling comfortable in my skin in a way I never had. It wasn't because I had changed anything about myself or grown in my ego. I simply was learning about Jesus. He changes everything, including our internal desires to measure up. I no longer felt like an exile. I belonged to Jesus.

My love for reading and learning exploded even more during my time as an RD. I felt like God was pushing me toward understanding further how to live out faith and learn about how to lead people better. My coworker Chris was an MBA graduate and convinced me to pursue my own MBA. The selling point for me was coming to the perspective that I didn't have to fit into a preconceived, profit-driven mold for business. I wanted to learn about how organizations are run, how to motivate and develop people, how to resolve conflict, how to communicate and market, how to manage finances, and everything this entailed. I learned business is relevant to everything, so there must be a way to serve in a Christ-like, restorative manner. *Anything can be ministry.*

Being an RD was teaching me so much more about diversity. I was learning more about backgrounds, politics, and different theologies from students and peers. My coworker and friend Momo taught me so much about life as an African-American female. *How does the church care for our communities? How do we point to Jesus, genuinely meet needs, and build relationships?*

Working at Waynesburg gave me the opportunity to lead a trip to Jamaica and experience another new culture. I had the opportunity to visit my friends Mick, Andrea, Audrey, and Emily out in their new home in gorgeous Los Angeles. This family has taught me so much about Jesus, unselfishness, and listening to the Holy Spirit. I'm so thankful for the continuing opportunities to experience life with incredible students and peers. I learn a little more about Jesus through each one.

The Foundry

(Playlist songs 45 - 47)

Not long after I started working at Waynesburg, I got in touch with childhood friends, now married, Rob and Kristi. Rob and Kristi were a little older and had been working for several years in full-time church ministry. I learned they were moving back to Morgantown to help plant a new church called The Foundry. I was focused on making RD life my ministry, but I still felt in the dark as to whether God was ever going to open a door to work with a church. My taste for churches was still bitter after the year I had been through. I still wondered what a true thriving church could look like. Rob posted an event for a pre-launch interest meeting in Morgantown. The concept for the church intrigued me. I had nothing to do and decided to go attend.

I remember my heart pounding driving through the rain to go to this meeting in the basement of another gracious local church. *Why am I freaking out?* Driving down the crowded strip of town I think I realized how daunting a task of starting any ministry in the city of the top ranked party school would be. I went in and met up with Rob and Kristi. It had been years since we had caught up. Rob introduced me to the Lead Pastor Justin and his wife Kara. Justin and I instantly hit it off. He's maybe the funniest guy I've ever met, but I was impressed with his heart and the vision for the church. These types of meetings continued in following weeks, and soon we started meeting over meals. I had become very intrigued by the church. I had no expectations for being involved. I lived a half-hour away. But, something was striking a chord and felt special. The vision for The Foundry was to be a life-giving church. This vision meant the church is passionate about the local community's needs, committed to outreach, and centered on relationships. I shared my heart for ministry with Justin and how I never wanted anyone to ever feel invisible at church. Every person who comes to church deserves to know they are truly valued. How does a church reflect Christ if this isn't true? The church ought to be the most welcoming, hospitable place on the planet. Jesus forgives the worst of sinners; therefore, everyone should be welcomed into this eternity altering relationship. To my surprise, Justin and Rob asked me to join the staff.

It's easy to look back with fond memories, but the following months were filled with doubt and stress. We tried spreading the news around as much as we could. For instance, we began what has become an annual tradition of handing out hot chocolate on Thanksgiving night to Black Friday shoppers. I was excited to be a part of developing a nonprofit organization built from scratch.

The more time goes by, the more and more details I'm learning it takes to run any organization. We began talks about location, finances, volunteer systems, website, partnership development, small group opportunities, community outreach, generational needs, church styles, church perceptions and stereotypes, societal injustices, etc. We committed to a culture of constant improvement, and therefore, these topics have continued to be evaluated and improved throughout the years. As a staff, we committed to always keeping everything about Jesus, dropping our egos and agendas and loving each other. The relationships I have built with this staff have been some of the best I have ever experienced (more on this in a minute). We had an initial loan and some outside support from a church planting network, but startup costs still seemed frightening. We made a commitment to be a church that dreamed God-sized dreams. This was one area where Justin, Rob, and I really were kindred spirits and had similar influences. We committed to praying to God to provide what He was calling us to do. God, if anything, blesses the furthering of His Kingdom. Why not walk in confidence of that?

After looking at several options, like a weekly set-up and tear down plan, we signed a lease on the bottom floor of an architecture firm just off the most popular street in town, including the best restaurants, bars, and clubs in town. We had previously set a date for starting preview services only a month away. This space was old offices, hallways, IT rooms, etc. Justin believed it had so much potential. I thought it seemed impossible. People started coming into the fray to help. Matt was looking for a church, and being an old bandmate, I connected him with Justin. Those two hit it off, and Matt was brought on to lead the music teams. Simultaneously, when Justin and Kara moved to Morgantown, another team from Texas moved to Morgantown to start a chapter of an affiliated campus ministry called Chi Alpha. We hit it off with them and committed to supporting each other. So many people helped us in a month's time completely renovate our floor of the building. We tore down walls, painted everything, installed audio equipment and projection TVs, built a cafe area and a stage with pallet walls and LED lightbulbs. I didn't have the slightest clue what I was doing, but Justin and Rob had a plan. *If we pull any of this off, it must be God.* Somehow everything came together, and we started doing church. We have tried to remain simple with times of worship through music and preaching expository messages (talks rooted contextually in scripture). We've endured plenty of growing pains, but we had incredible opportunities to ask ourselves every week how do we best love people and offer opportunity every week for people to begin and grow a relationship with Jesus.

Another commitment from the start was to be a place where everyone could have purpose and opportunity. If we really value everyone, we should care about their development. Faith is meant to be lived out, not just believed. A motto our staff has clung to is, "Always work to replace yourself." When more people can feel ownership and passion in following Jesus, the more they can feel alive, and ministry will exponentially grow. In addition to Matt, our friend Derrick from college came on to help lead our youth ministry. Not long after, our childhood friend Lori, like Rob and Kristi, decided to quit a paying ministry job to move back to volunteer in starting our children's ministry with a passion and belief I had never seen for children before. We brought on one of our originals from prelaunch days, Ashley, to be an administrative assistant and accountant. My mother became my MVP in hospitality, helping everyone feel loved, seeing small details and needs. My mom was impacted by the church and helped us build an environment of family. My mom is one of my heroes, and this is one example of how she lives selflessly. This is exactly how we wanted the church to live out. We met a guy named Chris who ran a local frozen yogurt shop. He came on to help us with media and has faithfully committed to studying scripture and doing life with people. Chris even saved me from dying from a heatstroke at an outside conference in D.C., but that's a hilarious story for another day.

What God has done in and through our church has been nothing short of remarkable. The building feels like a home and a refuge to me, but only because of how I've experienced the love of Jesus and the people inside it. Justin has become one of my very best friends because of his mentorship, his nonjudgmental respect in discussing literally anything, and his care in the hardest of moments. Our church has grown exceptionally well for a young church, but I've learned numbers are a misleading success metric. What matters is the stories of people's lives being changed for the better, stories of discovering Jesus and creating real friendships to help them through the hardest of experiences. Rob and Kristi moved and took a new exciting opportunity after a year, and my role transitioned from mainly guest assimilation into more of a pastoral role. Justin helped me begin the process of getting initial ministry education and credentials. I've met some amazing pastors, authors, and leaders who have encouraged me along the way. I've been grateful for the opportunity to share about Jesus in environments where I can talk about our history, the Gospel story, and helping people find the right opportunity to serve and live their passions in following Jesus.

I think the biggest area our church has succeeded in has been in caring for people. The clear majority of testimonies we've heard from people go along the lines of this: "When I came here, I immediately felt like I could be myself," or, "This felt like home in how people cared for me." We've fought to be a community that loves each other, and I think we have a start. Personally, I can testify to how amazing the church has been for my family. Not long before writing this book, my father left my mother. It has been the most unbelievable, painful, and confusing season. The way the church came around my mother, brother, and I is nothing short of a Godsend. This affirmed everything I believe in.

As a church, we are continuing to ask questions and dream big. We are dreaming of a day where we can have multiple expressions throughout our community. We want the church to be empowered to follow Jesus into every corner of real life. We are seeking how we can partner with existing, diverse community ministries and organizations. We dream of providing spaces, potentially businesses, for "something to do" for youth, college, and adult populations, for example. We want to create life and culture. I'm thankful for different conferences and networking opportunities we could glean from, and I'm dreaming of helping people receive similar transformative experiences. We want to see real needs, real issues and bring the salt and the light of Christ to them. I never dreamed I'd be a part of a family like The Foundry Church, but I'm beyond excited for the future as we're seeking after God's dreams and His scriptural mission for our city and beyond.

CHAPTER 9

Parting Thoughts - Life More Abundant

(Playlist songs 48 – 50)

I meet students every day who believe there isn't much purpose, meaning, or even hope in their lives. I've come to believe that the Gospel provides the hope for everything. Jesus changes everything. I'm asking a lot of different questions now. I've made peace with many issues I had throughout my life: *Do I belong? Am I worthy of love? Is life worth living? Is there a way back from pain and mistakes? Is Jesus real and does He really love me?* Now I'm learning and asking how we (fellow believers) can help others answer these same questions. It's been said that like the early history of the Christian church who lived in oppressive circumstances, the global church is living in exile. It's been well-noted how we in the western world are living in a post-Christian, post-modern society. I would agree with the thought we have always been in exile. Our truest, ultimate home is the Kingdom, is Heaven with God. I really like the thought. We should live knowing we are aliens, ambassadors, exiles. I'm asking, how do we reflect Christ in loving people and seek to bring reconciliation in this world? The presence of sin and the devil will always bring tension into this world to believers, but the church also hasn't always helped its case. The church has perpetrated or been indifferent to issues of poverty, racism, politics, human life, science, mental health, and more that are often real, merited concerns for all people. I believe Jesus wouldn't run from these issues but be present and sensitive. I'm asking how the church can be more present in real issues and yet still be true to the truths of scripture.

There are people far smarter than me who can answer many questions better than I can. I've listed many resources I've learned from in the back. If you get nothing else from this book, then get this: I encourage you to seek to experience Jesus for yourself. Search the scriptures for yourself. Ask your own questions, find resources, and try to see Jesus in your own life. I wrote this book not because I have new thoughts per se, but because in describing how I sought God in the highs, mundane, and lows of my life, you would be intrigued to do so for yourself. My life changed unbelievably when I chose to go all in with God. It had nothing to do with gaining anything, but simply saying, "Jesus, I have screwed up this life so bad; please write this story how you want now." And I believe he has redeemed my story for His glory. I learned this life is not my own. I have no idea where he'll take me. I have dreams about traveling, more education, entrepreneurial ideas, etc., but God always has the best in mind. This is the pattern seen in scripture, and I encourage you to discover that for yourself. There is literally nothing important to lose.

The joy of knowing and identifying with Jesus changed everything for me. He went around saying He is the Messiah, and He was the only way to God. Salvation is the craziest thing; how do we not deserve separation from God? The Bible is one giant love letter to us. We can live more alive than ever with the hope of now and eternity. I think a lot of times, people confuse these truths as an excuse for self-indulgence, self-centeredness. Let me make a clear point: Following Jesus is not about us. It's not always going to be easy. The Gospel is not one of "prosperity." It's not a free and easy ride to riches and heaven. We're still in exile remember? Jesus himself said the world hated Him, and don't be surprised if it hates you, too (John 15:18). The prosperity God wants to grow in us is the Fruits of the Spirit — love, joy, peace, forbearance, kindness, goodness, faithfulness, gentleness, and self-control (Gal. 5:22). These lead us in relationship with Him to a life of purpose and meaning. We can live each day with a mission and a great privilege to follow Jesus. We can love people and bring eternal impact. I think this is living out the "life to the full, the life more abundant" Jesus talks about in John 10:10 (KJV). I firmly believe in the "God shaped hole" concept. Whether we realize it or not, only Jesus can satisfy the longings we have; only He can forgive the sin in our lives. Sin is like a cancer that affects everything. It's a condition we can't overcome on our own. We can't earn our way out, and we're no better than anyone else through our attempts. We cannot do it without Him. We will experience the most joy, peace, and satisfaction when we "die to ourselves" and see God glorified, not ourselves.

Connecting Faith and Life

Worshipping God is about how you live. Worship is about realizing who God is and who we are because of Him. Worship is putting Him in His rightful place as Lord and King of our lives. Worship is saying thank you. Worship is a soul deep experience of knowing Him and being in awe and adoration. Some people may only associate the idea of worship with music. This is a narrow view. Worship matters to every area of your life. It's about perspective. Do we realize how lucky we are to be alive and to have any of the things we have? Do we still choose to have joy and praise God for who He is when circumstances are difficult?

Worship starts with looking at the different aspects of life. What relationships in your life can you celebrate and be thankful for? How has God been faithful in providing hope where there are difficult relationships? I think relationships are a huge way to worship God. Jesus talked relentlessly about compassion and loving your neighbor (everyone) like you love yourself. I think in any context it's important to find those with pain or without friends and truly care about them. I don't mean only small token acts of kindness (not bad), but I mean taking the time to appreciate and dignify people. The early church was known for "giving to each other as they had need" (Acts 2:45). I think this worship would change the world.

How can your work be worship? Most people aren't called to vocational ministry (still equally important), but that doesn't make your work any less important, ordained, or ministry. God calls us into every square inch of this Earth. When you go to work, you "go" to a ministry. Your passion, effort, and heart all can reflect Christ. You build relationships in your work sphere. You may think your work is completely unrelated to God's mission, but this isn't true. God called us to "be fruitful and multiply" (Gen. 1:28). Building communities and working were God's idea and plan for us in the first place. Work is a holy privilege. Whatever you do, whether you provide a service or a product, there probably is a way of benefitting society and honoring God in how you do it. This is the redemptive perspective, because we know many things can be corrupt and sinfully contaminated. Know that your work and passions matter to God. You aren't wired how you are by accident. There's an amazing movement called Business as Mission (BAM), which focuses on entrepreneurial community development, which helped me put this in perspective. Lifelong learning is so important within this idea. There is so much to discover about Jesus as we live daily life and keep life in eternal, Kingdom perspective.

Seeing Christ through culture was an important aspect of developing my faith. I once heard a story, which is famous and has been recounted in many ways elsewhere. The story goes that the authors CS Lewis and J.R.R. Tolkien were having a conversation while they both worked at the University of Oxford. The conversation centered on the relevance of Christianity, and Tolkien compared it to myths or stories (a place of belonging, see chapter 1). Lewis understood the power of myths and the joy and emotions they provoke but felt ultimately, they are "lies breathed through silver." Tolkien countered that most myths aren't full lies but instead are essentially "echoes" or shadows if you will of the truths God spoke into the world from the very start and are in many ways misguided or incomplete. In the beginning, there was only joy and peace with God. We all long to return to that fulfillment. The emotions and longings we experience from art, myths (stories), and experiences Tolkien referred to as "memories of creation." These memories (echoes, shadows) we find in "myths" are calling us back to the true fulfillment of the Gospel. This conversation was instrumental in Lewis' conversion to faith just days later.

God is the embodiment of creativity. Everything, though often misguided in a sinful world, points back to Him. If you think God is boring, then I would bet you have only experienced boring churches or perspectives. Look around at how incredible nature is. The scriptures are filled with music and art. God came up with these. God is the orchestrator of things like the laws of science and of sound. I believe you can experience God's goodness and worship Him through whatever your passion is: Music, art, film, science, sports — anything! An example I've seen of living this is through my old boss and friend Luke. Luke runs an MMA training camp out in a Philadelphia suburb where participants train for fitness, and some take on amateur tournaments. Every part of this camp involves personal development, and practices involve Bible studies and discussions. Luke has built a family atmosphere, and people are growing closer with each other and Christ while sharing a love for MMA.

Culture helped me understand spiritual concepts and make more sense of God at work in my story. I've noted how different music helped me through difficult times but also made me ask questions. Different music caused me to wonder if there was more to life than I was experiencing, if I was living a shallow and mistake prone life, and if there was a God who wanted an intimate relationship with me. The crazy thing is often it wasn't "Christian music" which sparked this. It was more about being introduced to ideas and personally seeking after God. The music which eventually spoke to me and enriched me though is the music which pointed me toward Jesus.

In the same vein, different films helped me to seek after Jesus. These weren't Christian films at all but often incorporated spiritual (sometimes Christian) concepts, which stirred things within me. I learned to see Jesus as the answer to the longings I discovered through these films. All my life I've been a sci-fi movie fan. I'd watch *Star Wars* or *The Avengers* and know intrinsically there is a battle of good vs. evil in the world. I think the example of Luke Skywalker teaches a lot about leaving your past behind, knowing you were meant to live for something greater. This theme also is prevalent throughout the 2009 reboot of *Star Trek*. This helped push me out of complacency. The movie *Avatar* moved me so much when it came out during my college freshmen year. I longed for a world where life seemed new and pure. I longed to trust there is a God who hears me and answers prayers. The show *Lost* taught me the importance of community ("no one does it alone"). *Lost* taught me about redemption, forgiveness, and inspired me to search the scriptures to see how God radically changes lives for the better (as well as dream of visiting Hawaii, but I digress). In high school, I watched the movie *The Bucket List*, and it taught me life isn't about me, and joy is found in giving someone else a better life. These films all introduced concepts where I could search the scriptures and discover more about God. I encourage you to see culture through the same perspectives to have an appreciation for creativity and to learn to think biblically about everything.

Our Hope

When we follow Jesus, we now belong to a family. A family we invite others to be adopted into. I chose to believe Jesus is who He said He was. The scriptures talk about heaven, and hell, and a lot about living in the here and now. There's many perspectives about the Bible, but I find peace in reading how Jesus took the scriptures seriously as God's Word to us and as Truth. When we follow Jesus, our soul prospers (Fruits of the Spirit). We can experience the "life more abundant" here and now (John 10:10, KJV). Jesus can heal our personal and societal pains. He is our hope for reconciliation. Nothing can separate us from this love (Rom 8:38). Life isn't about what we can gain. Our experiences are gifts from God and reflect His goodness, but we have a mission bigger than ourselves.

We are called to love God and love people *as we love ourselves.* If only we realized the weight of this and even achieved a small measure of action, the world would be forever changed. A few Bible passages have helped me understand this mission. The first is the message of reconciliation we are charged with in 2 Corinthians 5:11-21. A passage which compliments this well is Jeremiah 22:3, which says, "Thus says the Lord: Do justice and righteousness, and deliver from the hand of the oppressor him who has been robbed. And do no wrong or violence to the resident alien, the fatherless, and the widow, nor shed innocent blood in this place." The final verse is John 13:35, which says, "By this everyone will know that you are my disciples, if you love one another."

Following Jesus may bring pain, even the literal loss of our lives. We do have to remember there is a real devil out there who wants to destroy us. Jesus talked about losing your life to truly find it (Matthew 10:39). This life isn't about us, and realizing that will bring the most joy. There's much to understand, and this side of eternity won't bring clarity to everything, but scripture promises His Glory will overshadow any temporary hurt. We can take the good and bad in our lives and let Jesus leverage them for His purposes. We are never given anything for only of own gain but to give, restore, and reflect Christ. We can have a daily relationship with the Holy Spirit and let Him lead our lives. We have no idea where He will lead us, but I really believe it will be better than anything we can do on our own. We can trust God is good. Jesus changed everything in my life. I was lost, but He saved me in many ways. You can experience all of this. Your life matters, and you are not insignificant. You live in this world, and you are free to truly live. Jesus can save you and change your entire existence. There's nothing important to lose by accepting His forgiveness and starting a relationship with Him. We may be exiles, but we were made to belong to Him. We are called to join His church of people seeking to love Him and love each other. He never leaves us nor forsakes us, and we when we follow Him, we have the hope of forever with Him.

RESOURCES

Different forms of resources have impacted my life, and I would love to share those. I highly recommend:

Books/Magazines:

The Bible - This is the non-negotiable. A good start is having a study Bible. I like the Fire Bible and the Jesus Bible, but ask around for other perspectives, too.
Relevant Magazine
"The Reason for God" by Tim Keller
"Multiply" by Francis Chan
"Passion: Bright Light of Glory" by Louie Giglio and others
"Mere Christianity" by CS Lewis
"A Mile Wide" by Brandon Hatmaker
"Searching for God Knows What" by Donald Miller
"Fearless" by George O. Wood
"Jesus Is_" by Judah Smith
"5 Years to Life" by Sam Huddleston
"Crazy Love" by Francis Chan
"In a Pit with a Lion on a Snowy Day" by Mark Batterson
"Man's Search for Meaning" by Viktor Frankl
"The One Jesus Loves" by Robert Crosby
"Called" by Mark Labberton
"Through the Eyes of a Lion" by Levi Lusko
"Blue Like Jazz" by Donald Miller

"Scary Close" by Donald Miller
"Live Love Lead" by Brian Houston
"Do You Want To Change Your Life" by Greg Laurie
"The Purpose Driven Life" by Rick Warren
"Love Does" by Bob Goff
"Good Faith" by David Kinnaman and Gabe Lyons
"I Am Not But I Know I Am" by Louie Giglio
"I Am Second" by Doug Bender and Dave Sterrett
"The Cost of Discipleship" by Dietrich Bonhoeffer
"The Pursuit of God" by AW Tozer
"The City of God" by Augustine
"Sit, Walk, Stand" by Watchman Nee
"Let Hope In" by Pete Wilson
"Words from The Hill" by Stu Garrard
"Simply Christian" by NT Wright
"Life Is_" by Judah Smith
"Business as Mission" by C. Neal Johnson
"Toxic Charity" by Robert Lupton
"Let Justice Roll Down" by John M. Perkins
"With Justice For All" by John M. Perkins
"Every Good Endeavor" by Tim Keller
"Power for Life" by Jeff Leake
"It's Not What You Think" by Jefferson Bethke
"Just As I Am" by Billy Graham
"Sandcastle Kings" by Rich Wilkerson Jr.
"Start" by Jon Acuff
"LA Justice" by Bob Vernon.
"Ask It" by Andy Stanley
"Sinner's Creed" by Scott Stapp
"Delirious" by Martin Smith
"The Key to Everything" by Matt Keller
"Visions of Vocation" by Steven Garber
"Refining Fire" by Duane Eastman
"9 Disciplines of Enduring Leadership" by Kent Ingle
"Fight" by Craig Groeschel

"Contagious Christian" by Bill Hybels
"Unashamed" by Christine Caine
"Wine to Water" by Doc Hendley

To my surprise, I have found many theology textbooks to be easily readable and rich in information. They have been incredibly important in my growth. Do some research to find good ones, or hit me up on social media for my suggestions.

Music:

Hillsong United, Phil Wickham, Delirious/anything by Martin Smith or Stu G (personal favorite), Lecrae, Passion worship, The Beatitudes Project, and a bunch more mentioned in the book.

Other Media:

The Bible miniseries
I Am Second
Alpha Course/ Film Series

ACKNOWLEDGEMENTS

Thank you, Jesus, for never leaving me or letting me rot after all the mistakes I have made. I learn more everyday how your love isn't conditional, and you are a reckless forgiver. You sought me out when I was far way — when I was in exile. Thank you for rescuing me into your love.

I'd like to thank all the people that have believed in me and supported me throughout the years when I did not feel worthwhile or lovable. This book is about the hope I found. Thank you to my amazing family. Thank you, Mom, for giving everything to care for Alan and me. You are the greatest. Thank you, Alan, for being the best, realest and funniest brother ever. Cool your jets (fuel melts steel beams?) on the conspiracy videos. I'll forever think I'm better than you at *FIFA*. Dad, this is hard, but thank you for all you did to provide and care for our family growing up. I hope one day we can be reconciled. Thank you, Frances, Sam, Bill, Char, Dan, Cindy, Gary, Kaitlyn, Riley, Billy, Andrea, Kenny, Carlo, and Madonna! Thank you to my grandparents Bill and Ruth; I miss you every day. Thank you, Lauren, for being my best friend and the greatest example of Christ I've ever met.

Thank you to my family at The Foundry Church. Thank you, Justin, for always listening and pointing me to God's heart. I am who I am in large part to the years I've been able to learn from and do life with you. Matt, thank you for being my bandmate and friend since college. You helped me to keep going and to keep believing. Thank you, Kara, Derrick, Rob, Kristi, Lori and Dan, Chris, Ashley and Jordan, Rich and Ashley, Jess and Drew, Eric, Hannah, Alisa and Brad, and countless others at church for living out a Christ-like community. Thank you to my Chi Alpha friends Jordan, Katie, Katy, Charles, Chris, Sean and Heather for being so committed to loving the students at WVU. You are a light.

Thank you so much to all the people who've invested in me as a student and then while working with me at Waynesburg. Thank you, Dave, Sned, Luke, Blair, K, Evan, Warner, Jaclyn, Katie, Rachel, Spenser, Kylee and many more peers who helped me as a student realize I was loved. Thank you, Chris, for always being there encouraging me to come back to work, and letting me coach lacrosse with you. Thank you, Chris and Kelley, Jim, Josh and Jess, Carolyn, Russ, Bailey, Matt, Laurie, Emily, Ashley, Momo, Chaley, Pat, and so many more who believed in me as an RD. Thank you to all the amazing students I've met at Waynesburg as an RD. I love you all.

Thank you to all my childhood and high school friends; you all know who you are, and I am thankful for each one of you.

Thank you to all the mentors and pastors that have invested in me. I'm thankful for you and will always remember all of you.

Thank you, Red Pandas and cats. Thank you, Chris Jericho. Thank you, Concord grapes.

Thank you, Dan Kephart, for helping edit and shape this book. The world will someday love your writing! Thank you, Megan Fox, for your work in editing this book. You completely "get" this book and helped it come to life. I'm forever grateful. Thank you to the amazing team at WestBow Press for helping this book become a reality!

And thank you to you, the reader. This book is for you. God bless.

ABOUT THE AUTHOR

Anthony is a staff pastor at The Foundry Church in Morgantown, W.Va., and a resident director at Waynesburg University in Waynesburg, Pa. Anthony holds an MBA from Waynesburg University and is currently pursuing an MA in ministerial leadership from Southeastern University in Lakeland, Fla. At Waynesburg, he mentors students, teaches courses, and works on the campus ministry leadership team. He has also coached men's lacrosse. Anthony is credentialed in the Assemblies of God.

Anthony is thankful for the different struggles God brought him through in his life because now he gets to help people through their own. Anthony loves books, music, movies, video games, MMA, pro wrestling, good beaches and mountains to name a few things. Anthony wants his life's legacy to be about sharing the hope, peace, and salvation found only in Jesus (Romans 5 & 6).

47687678R00078

Made in the USA
Middletown, DE
31 August 2017